Building

the most

Effective

Sales Force

in the World

the era post the global financial crisis

Adele Crane

Revised Edition 2012

First published in 2009

Revised edition published in 2012

National Library of Australia Cataloguing-in-publication data:

Building the Most Effective Sales Force in the World:
the era post the global financial crisis

ISBN: 1449960359

ISBN 13: 9781449960353

Distributed by: CreateSpace, LLC, an Amazon.com Company
Cover Design by Marylands Creative, United States

Other Books and Publications by the Author:

Get Sales Focused:
Rethinking and Revolutionizing Sales Forces and Sales Results

Kirkus Reviews Say:

"A welcome update on building a sales force in the new economic environment"

The financial meltdown of 2008 claimed many victims, but an area that surely felt intense pressure was the corporate sales force. Every company's sales force had to adjust to a new market reality. The author of this timely book, an international business consultant who highlights some of her firm's research into sales organizations, writes that a "new customer profile" started to take shape after the financial crisis. Customers "were less trusting and found heavy selling tactics repulsive...they wanted price and if that was right, then they would look at other key factors." Crane says, "Effective salespeople now are those that are able to confront and challenge their customers' thinking and influence them in such a way that changes their minds." This new requirement, the author says, demands a new kind of salesperson: "It is about a sales force that is enabled with a broader degree of knowledge and skill that can take a strong case to customers and influence them to change their minds about how they do business." Crane offers important advice to companies, including how to refocus, why a new kind of sales manager is necessary, the importance of systems, keys to developing the right relationship between sales and marketing, and, perhaps most importantly, ways to transform not just the sales force but the manner in which the company does business. Rather than serve up a sugarcoated, lightweight primer, Crane delves deeply into the messy, complex world of corporate selling. She strongly lobbies for "embracing transformation from within," even though she makes clear that there are no easy answers. Of course, making a case for taking action is one thing; executing a plan of action is quite another, so it's helpful that Crane includes three pertinent case studies at the end of the book to show in detail how business' transformations can impact sales in today's market.

"Don't be yesterday's company in tomorrow's world," she urges.

While some business executives may find the author's assessment sobering if not downright depressing, this book provides the wake-up call many may need to stoke up their sales forces.

Reviewed June 2012.

Building the most Effective Sales Force in the World

About the Author

Adele Crane is a leading and highly respected international business consultant with over twenty-five years' experience working in Australia, New Zealand, North America, the United Kingdom, and South Africa.

Adele's consultancy work has produced results for literally hundreds of organizations with many different industries through change management programs and development of high-performance teams. She is arguably one of the foremost authorities on sales forces in the world today. Her success has received recognition in major media forums across the world, and through her keynote speaking she has shared the stage with some of the most recognized and successful CEOs. Her expertise in leading change and growth is widely relied upon and she is considered a thought leader.

She has conducted in excess of two hundred in-depth business reviews and developed plans that have assisted companies achieve tens of millions of dollars of top-line revenue and above industry-standard profits. Her sales leadership capability has been demonstrated many times over, personally delivering cultural change programs across many industries in 90–120 days with sustainable growth achievements of in excess of 40 percent. She has delivered more successful turnarounds in the past decade than any other known consultant in the world.

Adele is renowned for her extraordinary diagnostic skills of businesses and her ability to provide candid and in-depth knowledge that assists companies in making quantum leaps forward with their organizations. Chief executive officers and sales managers seek Adele's analytical capabilities when they are looking to transform their sales organizations to ensure the right priorities in their projects are established with a keen eye on the top-line and bottom-line profitability.

Prior to consulting, Adele was a very successful salesperson in her own right, learning the skills of selling in the tough world of commission-only selling.

Preface

For many companies, the challenges of the new markets are going to define who they are as organizations in the future and the positions they will take in the market.

For some, the last few years have been a battlefield they have never encountered before, and many of the lessons learned are those they have learned through trial and error, as there was no handbook on how to survive a global financial crisis.

Executives have come through the first stages of the recession, battered and bruised, but those that survived are now looking to the future once again. They understand that the market has changed forever and that some companies can actually define this era as the time that changed their businesses forever to a smarter and improved business model.

The customers have changed forever, as their buying criteria are reprioritized and their decision-making criteria have altered. Through the crisis, companies experienced long-standing relationships being replaced with commercial requirements that tore apart those relationships. Customers looked to other providers as they were pressured by internal mandates to strip costs. Many of those relationships between vendors and customers were lost as redundancies were rampant through companies. The output from the crisis was that many new opportunities for companies to sell to customers where the doors were previously locked tight.

The one primary lesson that has been learned as many companies have closed their doors is that the number of opportunities in the markets has typically diminished and only the most competitive and highly tuned sales organizations will win in the future. These organizations will not be those that are just tuning up the sales process, but those that that have the ability to take tactical plans and successfully implement them with a keen focus on top-line revenue and bottom-line profits simultaneously. They will be the organizations that understand that sales management no longer is just about people management and coaching—the responsibilities of the role go far deeper into the organization.

The expectations of CEOs have shifted for the sales organization: they seek more commercial and substantive outputs that manage the business of sales rather than the people of sales. They look for the legacy that was sales management of hype, egos, and laissez-faire leadership styles to be replaced with skills that can create world-class sales organizations that can drive growth and secure major market share.

These are sales organizations that are transparent, measured, and accountable; manage direct and indirect costs; and have frontline leaderships that are embedded in coaching, guiding, improving the standards of all individuals.

The impact of these changes on sales managers and sales organizations is significant, and through this book you will gain insight into how need to structure, manage, and lead their sales organizations in the future. It will provide you with a grounding in what the sales organization will be in the future and insight into world-class sales organizations.

Table of Contents

Chapter 1:
The Massacre That Was the Global Financial Crisis   01

  The crisis that was like a financial tsunami   01

  How organizations responded   02

  How sales forces were affected   04

  The second financial tsunami   06

  The new customer profile starting to take shape   07

Chapter 2:
The Long Tail That Is the Global Financial Crisis   09

  The unyielding comparisons of this crisis with the
  Great Depression   09

  The beginning of sales forces as we know them today   10

  The emergence of new business models   11

  The new salesperson   12

  The evolving role of the sales manager   13

Chapter 3:
A Time to Refocus   **15**

  The rise of business criteria   15

  Traditional views stifle sales development   17

  The new criteria of sales forces   17

  Sales managers that close the doors unwittingly   20

  The CEO's perception can hold you back   20

Chapter 4:
The Crisis for Sales Managers   **23**

    Priorities of sales managers   23

    Sales leadership styles that guarantee failure   25

    A major shift in thinking   25

    Defining what sales leadership actually is   26

    When age can define the culture   27

    The CEO's perception of sales managers   29

    When the past will not manage the future   30

    The cut-off point for sales managers   33

Chapter 5:
Shifting to Excellence in Sales Organizations   **35**

    What is the measure for 'how much change'   35

    Lessons learned   36

    Is a world-class team really relevant?   37

    The writing is on the wall   39

    Laying down the path ahead   40

    Getting ego out of the way   40

    When simplicity is a tripping point   41

    The disconnect between senior executives and sales   42

Chapter 6:
So What Are You Actually Aiming For?   **45**

    It is like finding a needle in a hay stack   46

    It is all a big misunderstanding   47

    The absolute truth about sales managers' capabilities   49

    The great cover-up   56

Chapter 7:
Working Out Who Will Drive the Bus   **59**

    Sitting at the crossroads   59

    It is a defining moment in time   61

    Choosing the right benchmarks   62

    Changing times-changing people   63

    Heading out west   64

    Fact or Fiction   65

    Who's driving the bus   68

Chapter 8:
Why Some Companies Take Unnecessary Big Risks   **71**

    It is all about security and status quo   71

    Focusing on the lowest denominator   72

    Cash flow dries up patience   73

    The same mistake over and over again   74

    Growing your own   75

    A generous promotion by the director -
    with consequences   76

    So what is down the left road?   79

Chapter 9:
Looking at It from a Sales Manager's Perspective   **81**

    What is the best-sized organization to engage in transformations? 81

    Capping growth CEO-style   83

    Who will get the role of sales manager in the new marketplace?   84

    Smart companies apply more stringent
    recruitment practices   86

    When existing customers are considered high risk   87

    Two consistent traits of problem businesses   89

    Opening the door of success   89

Chapter 10:
All You Ever Hear about Is Systems - We Are in Sales!   **91**

    Systems that put you on the moneymaking line   91

    Having the right systems   92

    Risk management demands systems   94

    CRM is only a diminutive element of systems   95

    When sales results can disguise impending disaster   96

    Putting a value on systems   99

    What takes priority defines the outcome   100

Chapter 11:
Sales Force Effectiveness - What Does It Really Mean?   **103**

    The disillusionment of the terminology   103

    The truth about sales force effectiveness   105

    The devil is in the detail and depth applied   108

Chapter 12:
People, People, People   **109**

    Laissez-faire leaders create cultural problems   109

    Identifying the telltale signs of cultural problems   110

    Identifying the culture of a sales organization   113

    How cultures are created   116

    Keeping focused on the outcomes   117

Chapter 13:
I Purchased CRM Software But They Just Don't Use It   **119**

    CRM fails big time for many companies   119

    The naked sales force   120

    We wanted black and now we want red   121

    Technology does not manage cultural change   122

Chapter 14:
Sales and Marketing - A Match Made in Heaven?   **127**

The chicken or the egg syndrome   127

Born from the same cast   128

Getting the relationship right   128

Is marketing aligned to the new marketplace?   131

Marketing effectiveness   132

Chapter 15:
How are you playing the game?   **133**

Which team are you playing for?   133

Winners and losers   136

Chapter 16:
The Business Case for Transformation   **137**

Projects that fall over   137

Stepping back and getting the real facts   138

No business case-no transformation   140

Timeline to complete the business case   140

What can be concluded from the final business
case report?   140

Chapter 17:
Getting the Project Set Right **141**

    Getting the transformation team right 141

    Establishing the project priorities 142

    Setting down the baseline 142

    Treating the right issues 143

    Avoiding false starts 143

    Keeping the focus simultaneously on the top and bottom line 144

    Creating the summary of all subprojects 145

    Putting your finger on the project "go" button 146

Chapter 18:
It's All About the Baseline **147**

    The executive way 147

    A new way of looking at measurement 148

    The baseline stumbling blocks 148

    Getting structure and process right 150

    The curse of the product manager 151

    Structure and systems show the way to make money 151

    Building to world-class standards rather than our-class standards 152

    Giving it a makeover and making money 152

    We learned to fail many times over and over 153

Chapter 19:
Managing the High-Performance Sales Team **155**

    Getting your license to drive 155

    Measurement does not improve performance 156

    Measurement assists in good decision making and people's actions 156

    Good managers make good decisions 1657

Chapter 20:
The New Customer Dilemma   **161**

Taking the acid test   161
The redundant seller   162
Are you learning on borrowed time   163
Hiring?—then bear this in mind   164
Invest in me, he says   165
The making of legends   166

Chapter 21:
Does the Transformation Affect the Wider Organization?   **167**

One step at time can create one mountain at a time   167
The balanced organization   168
Cross communication creates cross employees   169
Good communication supports good transformations   169
The unbalanced organization implosion   170

Chapter 22:
Train to Achieve the Gain   **173**

Who is likely to fail first   173
Improvement comes from individuals improving too   174
Front and center to success   175
Why buy a dog and then bark too   177

Chapter 23:
What Will Ensure a Successful Transformation?   **179**

    Transformation versus change   179

    A tough call to face in some change situations   180

    Embracing transformation from within   180

    Getting the timing right   181

    Who is on the bus with the driver   182

    Who Blocked the Change Process?   182

    The Collective "Yes"   185

Chapter 24:
Don't be Yesterday's Company in Tomorrow's World   **189**

    Today or tomorrow?   189

    Living in another world   190

Epilogue   195

Case Study

    Industry Practice versus Best Practice   197

    Reworked Over and Over Again   201

    Capacity planning versus legacy planning   205

Chapter 1:

The Massacre That Was the Global Financial Crisis

In 2009, sales managers across the world awoke to a new era of management. The markets had changed and a new game had begun with the onset of the global financial crisis in the previous year. Many sales managers had never experienced such significant change in a market, and most were unprepared for what was forced upon them. For many senior executives, this was potentially the biggest challenge they had faced in many years, and organizations began to reel from the impact of the financial crisis that surged across the world like rapid fire. Executives now clearly understood what a global economy was and how it affected organizations, from even a smaller business downtown to the major corporations.

The crisis that was like a financial tsunami

The crisis was like a tsunami, working with great strength and swell as it surged across the different countries. The impact was felt at different degrees according to what drove the economy of that country and region. Like dominos cascading across a desk, different industries experienced the effects at different times; however, by the end of 2009, the full effects had been felt. Construction had collapsed, since finance was no longer obtainable for many projects. Buildings in their early stages of development were scraped to the ground, as projects had no foreseeable future to be completed. Financial-related markets collapsed and market confidence had literally left the building. The ramifications were felt from motor vehicle markets, manufacturing, and importers to the retailer. For those involved in mining industries, it was like being in a movie theatre seeing the world around them change while sitting comfortably in their seats as their industry continued to grow. Some other industries were also temporarily spared from the tsunami that was the global financial crisis.

Organizations across the world sent the mandate out to all their management to cut costs—hard and fast.

Sales organizations saw their sales pipelines go into a state of collapse as companies stepped back from purchasing and were totally focused on cost cutting. If it was not needed today to fill current customers orders—then it was no longer on the agenda.

Organizations running on high levels of debt or finance were the first to tumble and leave the market. They were potentially in unsustainable situations due to the high debt-levels-to-service ratio, so the moment funding was withdrawn, the bell tolled the end of their lives. Those were the early-exit organizations in the recessions across the world, and they were in many cases gone by January 1, 2009.

The next layer of organizations to collapse were those that had some cash resources but were challenged as they watched their markets ravaged by competitors and disappearing customer bases. The mandate to cut costs tore deep into the functions of all organizations, and there were very few places left where any surplus spending could be found.

Marketing departments were suddenly faced with little or no response to their campaigns. Many were taking to market campaigns that were out-of-date to their competitors before the ink had even dried. Marketing people were challenged to find an edge—a point of difference that had any relevance to the market as the buying patterns and behaviors of people were rapidly changing and in fact changing forever. Most marketers opted for major price reductions to attract any customers left in the market. But this drove profit out the door and placed them in high-risk situations of not being able to replenish stocks as the line between overheads and stock became unvaryingly thin.

How organizations responded

For many of the remaining organizations looked at their supply-chains and moved to positions of no risk. Implementations of new information technology systems were placed on hold; manufacturing upgrades were de-prioritized, as organizations were not even getting enough orders to keep their existing machines busy. Those organizations that had signed major capital purchase agreements sought legal ways to terminate or suspend the agreements.

Those organizations that were selling enterprise resource planning (ERP) systems and other major investments or innovations were starting to succumb to the third wave of expired companies in the market. Where their sales contracts could be exited, the customers disappeared quicker than a flock of birds near a hurricane. The remarkable year they thought they were going to have just vaporized before their eyes.

Sales managers were left like deer staring into bright headlights, not knowing what was coming at them. How do you make decisions when you can't work out what the target is doing each week? Strategy or tactics were developed, but just as they got to the customers, the market had shifted again. Customers that were there today were gone tomorrow. I remember one client that was thrilled to receive an order for several million dollars worth of production equipment, which was the culmination of many months of hard work. The order was received in October 2008 and by January 2009 it was nothing more than a document gathering dust. The customer had disappeared and the sales team gazed miserably at a document that represented what was once a great moment for their company.

The financial controllers looked at the top line collapsing and again sent down the communication from the board and directors to cut even more costs. The knives were out and they were being sharpened to new levels not seen before. They were looking for savings that could support drops in business of over 40 percent in some industries in those initial months of the global financial crisis—immediate savings that would directly impact cash flows.

The first and easiest cut that had the most immediate effect on the cash flow was to reduce head counts. Business was slow and many of the companies had surplus employees for the task requirements, so the head-count cutting began. Marketing departments sat in fear as their divisions were unable to produce leads and generate business. They watched as people were extracted around them. Teams of twenty marketers suddenly sat as lone employees in empty offices with just one or two people there for basic marketing requirements. The operational personnel were removed as orders slowed and the production and handling requirements rapidly decreased. Administration personnel and those deemed the least popular in the sales team (i.e., those who had been underperformers for some time) all had numbers on their heads, indicating their departure dates.

Recruitment organizations went from being the suppressed organizations of the market where they could not even find candidates, to an immediate opposite of being inundated with calls from people looking for work. From having to beg and plead their case for a person to change roles, they were now faced with the dilemma of not even being able to place them.

Sales were down and costs were cut to match the decline in sales. For many, a little sigh of relief started to echo around the corridors that organizations may survive, but they tentatively watched news broadcasts to see what the next wave would bring. Personnel left in the company were apprehensive over any directives being given by management, as they feared they would be next if another external impact was felt on the business. Company cultures collapsed to survival mode.

There were restructuring of price lists and costs analyses undertaken to ensure some degree of profitability for pricing sales personnel were taking to market. Executives knew they were in a battlefield out there and that they had to compete with what was now pricing levels lower than what they had seen in decades. They needed to win sales, but profit became a luxury for many companies.

For many companies that had enjoyed an overly buoyant marketplace pre the crisis, where demand exceeded supply, they were suddenly dropped back to earth. I watched particular equipment providers that were previously hiring equipment at up to 200 percent over market value due to the shortage of available machines, that suddenly had to rationalize their pricing as there was an oversupply of equipment in the market and an undersupply of orders. Their high life had ended with a thud on the pavement. Their price-cutting was, in effect, only cutting the premium out of their profits and not cutting to the core of their profits like many other companies. The market rationalized going back to real pricing and this occurred across many industries. Others that were on thinner margins were reduced to dangerously low margins with high risks associated with non-paying customers.

How sales forces were affected

From a sales perspective, the salespeople that were servicing existing accounts felt a sense of security. New business sellers were the most exposed, as new business was just not on the global agenda.

For account managers, the first signs of corporate cocooning behavior became apparent in the market as organizations sought to work with vendors they knew and trusted. The cocooning phase is best described as when people return to what they know and trust and surround themselves protectively with people and vendors they have faith in. Sales managers across the world told their salespeople to stay close to their customers and service them. They needed to protect their accounts.

Those customers with excess stock holdings adjusted their purchasing requirements based on the changed order flows. This meant that orders were slowing back to the vendors and that the next layer of the domino effect had begun. The sales force saw fewer stock requirements, conservative ordering, and the onset of the 90–120-day payment plan on those orders placed. Along with all the other domino effects, there was also the booked-order domino effect, which was then shadowed by the nonpayment domino effect.

Sales managers continued to confirm the need to be close to the existing customers and nurture the relationships. They encouraged their teams to work on the loyalty factor to make sure the competitors could not get in around them and to be aware of any approaches or changes and respond accordingly. The sales organizations were mimicking their customers and actually cocooning with them. The promotion of the process and high priority of the customer relationship became the mantra of customer management.

For many sales organizations, this seemed like a sound strategy, but very few thought about the fact that as some of their competitors exited the market, new customer opportunities may well be available. Someone had to fill those customers' orders, even though they were smaller in size due to the market conditions. There were small opportunities to be grasped in the market, and only the managers with the market savvy were quick enough to see those gaps and move on them.

Many other managers believed the tsunami had passed, and they and their customers were cocooning. It was about mid- to late-2009 and the markets had settled into what was believed to be near the bottom of the cycle that had hit so strongly just twelve months prior.

Executives were cautiously satisfied that they had made the right decisions through the crisis to guard their organizations.

The second financial tsunami

What they were unaware of was that the second wave of the tsunami was about to strike. Wild weather and market conditions again awaited them. The strike would not appear on the share markets of the United States and Europe but rather on the balance sheets and profit and loss reports at the organization level. With reduced finance available and the need to repay debt quickly under bank demands, organizations had to respond.

The second wave came quickly and caught many salespeople and companies off guard. The wave came in the message of a mandate from organization directors and boards of directors to cut the supply-chain costs and demand the prices needed for them to be profitable. Yes, they had already requested discounting on orders, but now it was a permanent mandate across all the supply chain.

There was a great case of cost cutting in Canada with the gas-related industries, where one of the organizations sent out an email to all its vendors, thanking them for their support and advising them that they were required to cut all costs by 15 percent immediately. All supply-chain purchases were to be put out to the open market if the vendors were unable to meet the new pricing requirements. Their immediate responses were required.

For financial controllers the news was devastating. For sales managers there was a ray of hope on the horizon. For salespeople charged with selling new business their time had arrived again. It was the rebirth of their role in the company.

For account managers it was a day of reality they will never forget. As they picked up the telephone or jumped in their cars and headed to the customers, they could not believe the question that had been presented to them. When they arrived at their customer's places of business, they pleaded the case of loyalty and the longevity of the relationship. The customers said, "That was the old days. Times have changed. We need you to cut your prices. It's not me; it's a directive from above." The customers were divorcing their vendors if they could not meet the new demands.

The salespeople headed back to their managers to see if they could cut the full 15 percent. The instructions were, "Go back and negotiate a good deal that will not leave us out in the cold at 15 percent. Focus on keeping the relationship alive."

The new business salespeople sped down the highways and pushed their way onto flights, all the time feeling the world had sent them a gift. The door had opened to accounts they had never been able to access and it was their time to get in front of those customers. They had the instructions to negotiate good deals, but they also realized that with other salespeople knocking at the door, they would need more than just price to win the deals. They had to kick into sales mode and really work hard to win the business.

Another impact of the crisis was now to be felt in sales organizations. Many of the salespeople had developed their skills in good markets. They had been focused on customer relationships, added-value selling, and partnering with customers. All the mantras that were conveyed around sales for the previous ten years or so were often embedded in a slower, more gentlemanly sales process. Older, more experienced sellers had seen some changes over the longer-term years and knew how to close hard and fast, and quickly drew back on those skills. New business opportunities were available but the skills needed by salespeople were out of sync with the changing market.

The new customer profile starting to take shape

The problem arose, however, that customers were now of a different ilk. They were less trusting and found heavy selling tactics repulsive. They knew the closes and lines being used and were aware of the desperation of the vendors when they were applied. Salespeople bestowing the virtues of relationships and partnering were out, as customers were aware the only reason the conversation was happening was price. They wanted price and if that was right, then they would look at other key factors.

Many customers already had vendor relationships and good logistics in the supply-chains, but what they lacked were prices that met the companies' new supply-chain demands.

Sales managers now were feeling the full impact of the crisis on their teams as they had to secure sales with customers that had changed most things they knew and that were accepted in a market.

Some managers were successful and others tragically failed at the challenge.

The changing of the guard occurred as customers moved from traditional vendors to new vendors, competitors exited the market, and the dynamics of each industry changed forever. When organizations looked at their surviving customer lists, many saw only 40–50 percent of their original customers still purchasing; and even less, if you included the debtors' ledger.

The domino effect of the market was felt everywhere. The only survivors were often the ones with government and mining contracts or those with customers that actually paid. Organizations' employee numbers were cut to the bone and only the barest minimum remained in jobs to keep the organizations functioning.

Even today, there continues to be a slow leakage of organizations exiting the market and employee numbers reducing as some of the organizations feel the final pain at the end of the supply-chains. Those with cash resources that survived the early days may have slowly run dry through lower sales, higher debtor ledgers, and unrecoverable debts.

Sales managers are left gazing at their belly buttons, contemplating their future and wondering how they will respond in the new market that is nothing like they ever knew in the past. Some organizations have elected to replace their sales managers in an attempt to find new people with the initiative to respond to the market. The advertisements on all the job boards show a common statement: "Must be strong in new customer development initiatives."

Sales teams look to their managers, seeking assistance on what to do now. What they were doing before was no longer working. It seems that the game has changed so much that they are unsure what they are playing, and no one has sent them the new rule book.

With the economy settling to all-time lows across many markets, organizations are now asking "which way forward." The emphasis on strategy and implementation has returned as they seek some degree of consistency in their organizations' performance for the years ahead.

Chapter 2:

The Long Tail That Is the Global Financial Crisis

As 2011 slowly drew to a close, many organizations started to desire the shift from survival mode to growth as they looked around it was obvious that there were still challenges ahead. The crisis definitely had a defined start date; however, the finish date was arguable for many industries and individuals. Did it actually finish, or is there an unprecedented long tail that moves the global financial crisis to a way of being rather than a period of time in history?

The unyielding comparisons of this crisis with the Great Depression

The latest global financial crisis is often compared to the Great Depression of 1929, and the similarities are staggering. The Great Depression was a severe worldwide economic depression. Its timing varied across nations, but in most countries it started in about 1929 and lasted until the late 1930s or early 1940s. It was the longest, most widespread, and deepest depression of the twentieth century. The Depression originated in the United States, starting with the fall in stock prices that began around September 4, 1929, and became worldwide news with the stock market crash of October 29, 1929 (known as Black Tuesday). From there, it quickly spread to almost every country in the world.

The Great Depression had devastating effects in virtually every country, rich and poor. Personal income, tax revenue, profits, and prices dropped, while international trade plunged by more than 50 percent. Unemployment in the United States rose to 25 percent, and in some countries rose as high as 33 percent. Cities all around the world were hit hard, especially those dependent on heavy industry. Construction was virtually halted in many countries. Farming and rural areas suffered as crop prices fell by approximately 60 percent. Facing plummeting demand with few alternate sources of jobs, areas dependent on primary sector industries such as cash cropping, mining, and logging suffered the most.

Some economies started to recover by the mid-1930s; in many countries the negative effects of the Great Depression lasted until September 1945 when World War II started. This was a depression that lasted a period of up to fifteen years before a full recovery could be declared.

If you were a young salesperson in that era, you are now around one hundred years of age. There will be few people that lived the entire Depression in their working lives but a number of people that can remember their childhood during the Depression.

The beginning of sales forces as we know them today

The Depression changed how people did business forever, much like the crisis we are all experiencing in the modern world today. Prior to the Depression, many products were sold through storefronts, and customers would come to the stores or business locations to make their purchases. Communication to convey businesses' marketing messages was limited to print and radio (for those that had one), so people kept informed by travelling to stores or "downtown" to see what was on offer. Salespeople were site-bound and the outdoor salespeople as we know them did not exist. As the Depression spread, businesses had to take drastic action to sell their products. The Depression was the start of the outdoor salesperson—a salesperson that took the company's wares to the customers in a more formal manner, much like the old-time drifter. Customers were introduced to the constant of the door-to-door salesperson, and companies became totally reliant on those salespeople's ability to communicate their products to customers and get orders.

This was the beginning of professional sales forces for many companies and countries.

If you consider what everyone is experiencing now as the financial markets remain turbulent, the dynamics of the markets have changed forever. The long tail of the current crisis has many similarities to the one experienced during the Great Depression. It is long, it is relentless, and the recovery will only occur for many companies through applying an exact science of the highest standards of performance in many areas of their businesses.

What could have been a learning curve in the past could end up being the curve that sends the company into a tailspin.

The emergence of new business models

Organizational strategies have been difficult to put in place, as companies have been unable to predict markets and recovery timelines. Most were focused on survival and that was their strategy. How can they be there today and tomorrow—let alone next year? For many to deliver twelve-month strategies that remain relevant has been a challenge in itself. The only common theme among all companies now is the agreement that the future will be difficult.

In a recent survey my research consulting firm, Sales Focus International, conducted of chief executive officers (CEOs) regarding confidence in the market, many reported they were optimistic about the future and felt they had experienced some degree of recovery in their businesses. They were now looking for growth, shareholder returns, and the capturing of new opportunities that had arrived in the market.

When we looked more closely at their definitions of recovery, many confirmed they had changed their business models considerably and their strategies on how they went to market. They had made major adjustments to their businesses, enabling the recovery to occur. The businesses today were nearly unrecognizable to what the businesses were just a few years ago.

Some CEOs reported that the crisis had definitely made their businesses smarter and more versatile, which potentially would not have happened otherwise. Others had developed leaner and smarter ways of doing business and taken on methods within sales and marketing that would never have come up on their radar previously.

They all agreed that customers have changed their purchasing criteria and demands on their vendors. The retail sector had conditioned consumers to seek special event sales and now was constrained by consumers that only purchased through those special sale days. The 10–20 percent reductions that once lured customers to special sale days were no longer of interest to them, so greater offerings had to be made to draw them into purchasing now.

The battle of the online shopping medium has entered strongly into the market with the changes in currency values, and their business models are now forever impacted. Those that make the changes early will survive, and those that wish for the good old days will fall victim to the long tail of the global financial crisis.

The new salesperson

Over the years we have done extensive research on effective sales and marketing processes. In recent research we have seen a major shift in how effectiveness is defined for salespeople. For many years the conventional thinking was that effective salespeople were those who spent a lot of time building and cultivating relationships as this would lead to customer loyalty. Training programs and internal company mantras were heavily weighted in cultivating relationships. As noted earlier in this book, the loyalty factor has gone out the window for many customers as they adjust their businesses to changing demands.

Effective salespeople now are those that are able to confront and challenge their customers' thinking and influence them in such a way that changes their minds. This has significant impact on how salespeople are selected, trained, and managed across the organization. It is not a return to the heavy-handed tactics of old-time sellers whose primary skills placed emphasis on presentation, objections, and closing. It is about a sales force that is enabled with a broader degree of knowledge and skill that can take a strong case to customers and influence them to change their minds about how they do business.

Companies need great clarity about their offerings to the market, and how they are taken to market and conveyed by salespeople to customers. Customers are experiencing high levels of clutter and noise in their environments with overcrowded marketplaces, and companies need sales forces that can bring very distinctive and clear propositions to the customers and influence them. The customers remain in the market for a much shorter period of time now, and those taking their time to explain their offerings and build relationships will find themselves out sold by their competitors—if the competitors have adopted the new techniques.

Organizations need to consider the effect of these changes now has on the sales organizations as a whole and in particular the sales manager. If customers are changing their demands and buying patterns with vendors, and organizations are changing their business models and how they go to market, then sales managers must also change their entire business models within their sales organizations, reflecting the new ways to market.

The evolving role of the sales manager

Over the past few years, sales managers have had to make significant changes for a recessionary marketplace. The primary task of all management has been to cut costs, which is always the first directive from executive leadership when a downturn occurs. Sales managers have been required to cut hard into travel expenses, operating expenses, and head counts, giving them a new style of sales organizations to manage. The luxuries of the past have been curbed, and this has immediately challenged how the sales organization has gone to market, communicated with their customers, and managed the sales process.

This approach of cutting costs is a relatively simple exercise for management, with the greatest impact being on the people element rather than the concept of the task. For managers to reduce team sizes with people they have built relationships with can be a devastating task. To curb expense spending is an easier task that will at times result in loud noises from teams but is well accepted, given the state of the market. It is the lesser of the two evils in cost cutting.

Now the pressure for sales managers is about applying skills to grow business in the new emerging environment. The single greatest shift that has been seen is the change that, ironically, was related to the one seen through the Great Depression. In the Great Depression the salespeople were sent to the customers. They were placed out in the field to gather orders.

In today's world with the quality of electronic media available, salespeople have been asked to do the reverse, and now many are based back in the offices and work locations, reaching out to customers through electronic media and communication methods. Where salespeople were once hired across many different districts, you now see more centralized models that have had to adopt technology into their sales practices.

No longer can companies afford to fly salespeople to customers' businesses where margins have been reduced. The cost of sales far outweighs the profits made from many customers.

Customers' time has become more critical in the sales process, and many customers report that they don't have time to spend with salespeople in the relationship-building methods of the past. They need improved output from sales meetings that adds value to their businesses and doesn't confirm what has already occurred in the past. The salesperson toting specials listed on a sales sheet is reported to be one of the most annoying salespeople in today's market. This approach is an expensive method of marketing for the sales organization and time wasted to the customers, as they expect more refined communication methods to be applied to simple tasks.

The salesperson who was trained in relationships, product special offerings, route selling, and account management is fast becoming a redundant individual. Much like the salesperson known as the "heavy closer," the "nurturer" has been grouped with this stereotype as dated skills.

What everyone can be confident of are these four factors:

1. The market has changed forever.

2. Customers have changed their criteria.

3. Salespeople's skill bases must change to meet the market and customers.

4. Sales managers must adapt quickly and with great skill to the new markets.

Chapter 3:
A Time to Refocus

The market has set a new stage for companies to operate on, and it is a time to refocus on what companies are doing across the organizations. The global financial crisis has caused many companies to focus on surviving, but the shift has to be made to focusing on thriving. Companies that are focusing primarily on quarterly earnings will miss many opportunities, as their focus is short-term and their decision making is based on short-term thinking.

Companies that focus on the top and bottom line, simultaneously, are the ones that will shape themselves for the future as they will have eyes on short-, medium-, and long-term opportunities. As the economies in their regions strengthen, they will have the momentum for growth already in place.

Some companies have already commenced on that path as they create new business models and establish themselves on the new stage. They are improving their performance across all areas of the business, which is predominately motivated through cost cutting and seeking more efficiency.

The rise of business criteria

Pre the global financial crisis, business efficiencies were something that was spoken about and seemed to be a trend in business management. It was good business practice, but there was so much momentum in the market and profits being made that the need was neither critical nor urgent. If they added a few points to the bottom line then they delivered good business management. Business efficiencies were often quiet projects within an organization that gave people focus and purpose. The rise of lean manufacturing and six sigma all giving process to efficiencies and cost reduction.

Sales organizations were considered effective due to the high top line revenues being delivered and good margins, there was no reason whatsoever to look more closely at them.

The marketing machines of CRM (customer relationship management) software vendors convinced companies to embark on major software purchases and implementation projects, and that was the focus of most companies in relation to sales.

During the crisis, companies prioritized lean principles for their operational areas as a method of reducing waste, improving cash, and improving operational flexibility. Companies taking that approach were able to adjust more quickly to the new markets. The sales organization was just pushed to sell whatever it could and keep some revenue flowing through the door.

Interestingly, pre the crisis, many of the sales audits and reviews I completed demonstrated that the accepted efficiencies of sales force were to be working an effective three days per week. The balance of their time was spent on a myriad of unfocused non-selling related activities. This was not a trend for specific industries it was seen across many different industries, from construction-related businesses to technology companies, from manufacturing companies to import/distribution companies. The general consensus was that it was how sales forces operated.

On peeling back deeper into the sales organization, there was continual evidence of companies losing up to ten points of bottom-line profit in the way the sales forces structured, managed, directed, and engaged across the broader organizations.

If you took some principles from lean manufacturing and applied them to the sales organization, it often demonstrated that the capacity of the salespeople was well underutilized and the cost of sales was potentially 50 percent higher than it should have been. Although these companies were successful, they had the capacity to grow significantly when performance was managed.

The methods in which the sales organizations are managed are based on many inherited practices and are often seen as the way companies operate. People's exposure is limited to their industry and the few companies they have worked for, and that defines how they view the sales force.

Because a sales manager will invest most of his/her time in product knowledge, industry knowledge, and people management, very few specialize in business-based sales force improvement.

The need has not been there for many years with the lush markets that most companies operated in. The market allowed for complacency and a false sense of security in what they were doing as the results were coming in.

Traditional views stifle sales development

For many years, companies have viewed sales organizations as customer connections and the people that gained orders from those customers, be those large capital equipment sales, major infrastructure projects, or regular sales orders. These people's roles were to be effective communicators (the sales process), be personable (rapport) and professional, and in the ideal world, use the CRM software to document communications with those customers. They were measured on top-line revenue and margin, and that was the extent of their corporate responsibility in a business.

With the new era post the global financial crisis, the sales organization now has to be viewed differently. The obvious responsibility of top-line revenue and margin remains; however, it now must be a profit center in its own right. It must also be measured for indirect costs, process improvement, and its effect on the bottom line of a company. Most pre-crisis sales organizations had large costs on the bottom lines of companies that went unidentified, unmeasured, and unmanaged.

Now the responsibilities of the sales manager and the senior executives jointly have changed, and those requirements will be instrumental in the improvement of the sales organization and overall profitability of the company.

The new criteria of sales forces

The ability of a sales organization to bring in top-line revenue with margin no longer cuts it. The companies are too lean internally to carry the indirect costs that are associated with the operation of salespeople. It is not possible to achieve overall effectiveness for the organization as a whole if the sales organization is left to continue with its inherited behaviors of sales force management.

Over the past two decades I have been actively delivering turnarounds for companies that were distressed and required immediate top-line and profitability improvement. The process was delivered in 90–120 days with processes that ensured sustainability. In an interview on CNN during the crisis, I was asked what the key thing was that assisted those companies in rapid improvement. This was a question that had never been asked so pointedly before and certainly made me stop and think. The answer: systemization—being the focus and systemization of getting people doing the right thing, with the right momentum and frequency, in the right direction, consistently. Having the core business elements aligned so that any sales effort directly contributes to the top line and removes all indirect costs.

The interview went on to discuss sales management and how executives should work with sales leaders, and the need for more refined measurement of performance that will be the catalyst for more business conversations that allow for business improvement.

The concept of measurement and systems always sounds simple and most would say "that is what we do already." It all comes down to the interpretation of each word or reference and how deeply it is applied. Certainly having a more analytical approach is a contributor, but having a very acute sense of profitability is the primary driver. Sales for too long has been about personalities more than profit.

Following the CNN interview I received a very interesting call in my Chicago office from a young man just outside Dallas, Texas. His was a technical company and he was trained in engineering. He referenced the interview and then explained to me his situation with his company. He had taken over from a long-standing sales manager and moved into the position of sales leader due to his technical knowledge and strong feedback from customers. He found the interview confronting, as it was the exact opposite of anything he had heard in relation to sales. He rang to discuss a couple of points I had raised and sought more clarification of what was referenced (typical engineer behavior!).

After about fifteen minutes of chatting, he volunteered that the hardest thing he had found in his new role was the lack of information that provided a good grounding for meetings with his CEO.

He felt underprepared for the meetings and needed more substance for decision making. The company was suffering from the recession and he felt that decisions were made emotively, not factually. He needed to establish more facts so he was more confident in his judgment.

We chatted further and he requested that I meet with his CEO, and a Skype call was set up. His CEO was a strong person that had built a very successful company with distribution across North America. He was smart and quick thinking and was a person you would follow in a crisis. He had always run the sales force as a secondary stream to the business; products had led the way. He now was also frustrated, as the natural momentum that was his business for many years had been pulled away with the crisis. We discussed the need for more commercial substance in the meetings and he agreed that this would also give him more confidence in his decisions. It was not something he had considered until his sales manager had raised the point with him.

After the usual back and forth, I flew to Dallas and spent a couple of days reviewing the business and established a set of measurements that provided the information required. We put in place a project plan of recommendations and priorities of actions to improve in the sales organization over the coming six months that they could drive internally. The outcome after six months was increased top-line and bottom-line profit and improved processes in the business that ensured minimal indirect profit leakage.

The sales manager was an unusual catalyst for this process, as typically we would receive contact from CEOs in relation to sales organization improvement. Most CEOs make contact with a conceptual idea of what they want but don't have the detailed specifics. They are seeking improvement, as they can see the rest of the organization formalizing what it is doing and becoming more refined, sharper, and more profitable while the sales organization is still performing the same as ever with some top-line fluctuations.

I was speaking at a conference of CEOs in Arizona whose organizations were predominately mid-size with entrepreneurial leaders. They were all privately owned companies that were there to discuss business improvement.

They had grown to a point where the behaviors that had built the company were now starting to stifle its growth.

Sales managers that close the doors unwittingly

During the presentation there were the usual questions from the audience, but I noted a sense of quiet among them all when talking about sales managers and sales forces. They all agreed with what was in the presentation and understood the business value it would deliver to them. The more commercial component removing all the gray and mystic they found very appealing. During the open discussion time that followed the presentation, I asked them what they saw as the greatest challenge for them to embark on improvement of the sales organization. The general agreement from the audience was "talking with the sales manager about it." They felt that sales managers would not be receptive to the improvements and they were fearful of the repercussions, as they needed consistency in the top line. The subject was then discussed in more depth with the audience.

There were several points that stemmed from the group's thoughts of the receptiveness of sales managers. Firstly there was a major concern that the sales managers would fall back to the old-time stance of threatening them with customer and team fall-out. They were concerned that the sales managers would not have the time to implement the improvements and the team resistance might take away from sales revenue. They had attempted to make changes in the past and were not successful.

The CEO's perception can hold you back

I posed the question,

> *"Do you see your sales manager as a business manager or a people manager?"*

Those that categorized them as only people managers needed to reconsider the structure of the sales organization and put in place a business manager for the sales organization overseeing the people manager. Those that categorized them as business managers needed to consider if they interacted with them as business managers. Did they hold conversations about process improvement?

Did they hold conversations with them about risk management? What was the substance of their communication? Did the company's conversation really match the business requirements of the sales organization or was it narrowed to revenue, margin, product, and opportunities? Many reported they could see disunity between expectation and communication.

Some reported they had not wanted the sales managers involved in anything more than people and customer management but had not given any consideration to the wider impact they can have just by giving the sales teams directives. When it was discussed with more depth regarding how simple directives can create large indirect costs, they shifted their thinking to the requirement for commercial-orientated people.

To walk up to a sales manager that has been performing well over the years and suddenly announce that there has to be improvements would be considered boorish. If the sales manager had contributed to sustaining the business through the crisis, he or she would be perplexed by the statements.

If the discussions with the sales manager are moved to more commercial content and the need for refinement, process improvement (not narrowed to sales process improvement), and improvement related to competitiveness and more positive tones, it will be received in a far more receptive fashion. The business will be maturing rather than repairing. It will be raising the overall professionalism and value of everyone's contribution. It has to be a project of improvement, much like one that would be applied to a "lean methodology project" and not a victimization of their performance.

With the right understanding and communication, sales organizations can embrace the opportunities of improvement where the company culture is right. Throughout the book we will examine this more deeply.

Chapter 4:

The Crisis for Sales Managers

Sales managers have all been impacted by the crisis and have felt pressure and stress at levels they did not ever foresee as possible. They have been the stewards of teams that have experienced the worst crisis in living memory for many of their team members. The impact on those people is not just in sales figures but also in morale and self-confidence and in seeing long-term friends and coworkers terminated.

For some time, sales forces were able to relate the declining sales results to the market as the crisis escalated around them. For most of 2009, the results were plausible and valid and their experiences the same as their competitors. If they applied industry averages they were right in the thick of it. They were operating in market that was in freefall and no one really knew where the bottom of the market would actually be.

Sales managers that are out of touch with the market will often debate that there is still room for the skills that they and their teams have utilized for many years. They feel the struggle to get sales is just part of the recessionary market place. Other sales managers have identified the shifts or changes in the market and have taken action. There is also the group that has identified the need for change but they are grappling with the big question—"what do I actually change."

Salespeople going to customers with skills out of alignment to the market may be getting sales results, but often they are behind quota and still relating that performance to the marketplace. Those sales managers monitoring conversion ratios will be quick to identify whether the changes are market related or performance related. Those that are not monitoring conversion ratios deeply into the sales process are at best gambling with what the conditions really are.

Priorities of sales managers

What sales managers need to address is that the question "if the market will further change" is not a reason to stall; the market has changed forever and now the issue is over how to stay current in the new market and drive growth.

The change will continue and you need to be in sync with the market and no just following behind. The fact is, there are many issues to deal with from a sales manager's perspective.

Never before have sales managers been required to adopt new skills and knowledge as quickly as they are now being asked to by their organizations. Their skill sets are exposed more than ever before and the luxury of time is not on their side for slow changes to be made.

Sales managers need to consider that organization directors and boards of directors have reached the milestone in the minds where it is time to get companies moving forward again. They have survived and now they need to grow. Companies need to get back to the revenue levels and profitability they experienced previously and build the customer bases back up again. Those that are reporting to shareholders have a far greater sense of urgency to this than those that are owned by individuals or family-owned companies where they have had and continue to have a slower sense of timing to profitability. The leadership of such a company takes a longer-term look at things due to the sense of security that they own the company, whereas CEOs that are hired know that their life spans with companies are only dictated by the profits they deliver.

Chief sales officers, national sales managers, and similar roles are now confronted with designing sales strategies that will resurrect organizations' sales performance and drive the growth into the future. They look to their sales managers or front-line managers to translate those strategies at the customer interface and achieve the quota set.

Often provided with just a sales revenue and margin goal to deliver, sales managers are left to devise the implementation strategy that will deliver the required outcomes; the channels to market, the offerings to market, and the way the sales force will interact with the customers. If they get this just 5 percent out of alignment with the market today, it can mean disaster. Organizations do not have the buffer they have had in the past to accept or tolerate underperformance in the sales organization. They are heavily reliant on those results being delivered just to meet operational costs and earn moderate profits.

The implementation strategy of the new business model is required to be delivered with razor-sharp expertise and insightful attention to detail.

Sales leadership styles that guarantee failure

Sales organizations often known for their laissez-faire leadership will feel the highest level of impact over the coming years. For those unfamiliar with the expression of laissez-faire leadership, it is defined as a non-authoritarian leadership style. Laissez-faire leaders try to give the least possible guidance to subordinates and try to achieve control through less-obvious means. They believe that people excel when they are left alone to respond to their responsibilities and obligations in their own ways.

The issue with this leadership style is that you have sales individuals operating in a new market on a trial-and-error basis that attracts a very high cost of sales and high risk of failure. With the time constraints of how sales organizations must perform and the magnifying glass on sales managers' performance, an approach of leaving people alone when they are desperate for guidance is not plausible.

This does not mean it is time for micromanagement either. That would be the extreme in the other direction. Sales managers require very clear and defined implementation strategies for their teams that will deliver the results.

This may require a complete restructure of the sales organization, and with that comes the requirement for absolute and uncompromised sales force effectiveness. This is not associated with the narrow narrative typically applied to the subject of sales force effectiveness (the steps within the sales process) but with the broader view of everything that affects the sales organization.

A major shift in thinking

The most significant shift for sales managers is the first requirement to become more commercial in their thinking and not only manage business units that focus on delivering top line and gross margins. They also must now manage all the risks associated with customers, employees, knowledge, and all other contributing factors while bringing about market alignment. As you read through this book, I will elaborate further on all these points that are integral to the new sales leader's success.

With the changes occurring in sales organizations, it is now time for genuine leadership to be applied by sales managers. Salespeople are concerned over change, new directions, and certainly failure. Many will be required to learn new skills and practices and respond differently to customers. The changes in management styles for the sales organization is potentially one of the most dramatic changes that will be experienced for many years. Without good leadership, salespeople will become disillusioned and their experiences can be more traumatic as they struggle with the new markets.

The pressure on sales managers is not only from their employers but also from their teams. Many need to change their personal styles of management, learn new skills for guiding their teams in the market, and ensure sales organizations are in place that can deliver the outcomes.

Defining what sales leadership actually is

If we revisit what leadership is, it is essentially related to a person's skills, abilities, and degree of influence. Leading is the result of using one's role and leadership ability to influence others in some way. For sales managers it is the ability to influence people to take the journey of change to the new sales world that everyone must now operate in. Often leadership and management are confused; they are not the same thing. Management is getting things done through others. Leadership is getting others to want to do things. Leadership is intimately tied to motivating and influencing others.

True leaders are not bosses or commanders. They are not authoritarians that are seeking power over others. True leadership comes from influence, connection, reliability, and integrity. Successful leaders are committed to creating a world to which people want to belong—the sales organization. Successful leadership involves managing relationships and communicating within a team to move toward a specific goal. Leadership is the ability to express a vision, influence others to achieve results, encourage team cooperation, and be an example.

For many sales managers, this leadership style is a fundamental change in how they interact with their teams and in the overall operational requirements of the sales organization.

It certainly will directly impact how they deliver the organizations' strategies at grassroots levels. Strategy implementation is no longer a simple exercise of selling more stock to more customers, which is how many companies saw it in the past. Strategy implementation now requires a refined set of business skills, leadership skills, sales capability, and above all, detailed focus on outcomes.

What consistent element we do see is that every strategy involves new customer acquisition at a much more aggressive rate than ever applied in the past. Adding more complexity to this is the requirement of new customers through new sales channels (ways of reaching/connecting with customers). This is for many a new skill and one that has not been honed or developed. It is a difficult skill to learn in good markets, let alone in a market with strong competition.

If we look at the background of sales managers and how they evolved, we can better understand the responses they have to the challenges in the market and the journey ahead for them. Many have come from lush markets where the focus was on existing customers and building customer loyalty. New customer acquisition occurred but it was a secondary process to building the customer base.

When age can define the culture

Another overriding contribution to the challenges faced by organizations is the age of the sales manager. Each generation of sales managers has a different motivation, set of values, and beliefs about how sales forces should be operated. Where this is out of sync with the new market requirements, it creates an enormous amount of pressure for sales managers, as they are faced with making significant personal changes in order to be effective in the new trading environment. They are impacted by the need for change in themselves and their teams.

Combined with the generations are the different industries and practices adopted over the years. Those from high-commission sales environments commonly survive on new customers. Their ability to respond to the market for new accounts is much more readily applied than that of their counterparts who have come from industries with high reliance on existing accounts.

If we look at the different age groups, the trends of management methodologies appear. First, with all trends there are exceptions. It is important to keep this in context. Trends show mean averages. There are those that are close to the mean average and those that stand further away from it. The key to the following information is to understand the trend and where you sit within that trend, not just pick a category.

A large proportion of sales managers are in the category of baby boomers. The baby boomers (45–60+-year-olds) are heading into retirement and demonstrate resistance toward many of the modern business practice requirements. They operate on a high level of trust with their team and place all the emphasis on business relationships; therefore, they see no need for business process and reporting. They see themselves as the owners of customer knowledge and industry know-how, only sharing this as they deem necessary. They view a sales role as their personal value in the market and they pass on this attitude to the sales team, who also centralize their customer knowledge and selling process around themselves, not on a shared basis. These individuals operate to their own requirements within a business unit, believing that the business suffers each time the human capital mix is altered—thus producing a high reliance on customer relationships between an individual and an organization. This is the realm in which the mystic of the sales organization was born and developed. The tag of "it's an art form" grew from in this mentality. This is also where the expression of laissez-faire leaders was cultivated.

Baby boomers have a gift for keeping things verbal and fluid, which also leaves them with little ability to track their performance and keeps the sales organization as an art form rather than a science. Their reluctance to report is translated to the team, which is difficult to manage as it too adopts the attitude that sales is an art.

These managers have suffered the most in the global financial crisis, as they have had to make the hard decisions to terminate long-standing members of the sales teams. Many have taken a personal hit with their customers as they watched relationships disintegrating around them when their customers met their own organizational demands and reprioritized their relationships.

At executive meetings, baby boomers' conversations are limited to the old mantra about customer relationships and customer connections, and the underlying threat to management that "if I go the knowledge goes too." When asked for hard numbers and facts, they continue to use moving goal posts and verbal communication to work their way through the challenges.

The problem for the executives of companies is that these people are responsible for the revenue stream of the organization, and art does just not cut it. The risk is too great to have the organization settled in the hands of a few people. They need more facts and business discipline for the effective management-leadership of the sales organization.

The CEO's perception of sales managers

In a meeting of CEOs I attended in late in 2009, the issue of sales management was being discussed, and many who had previously (pre-2008) applauded the sales managers with this baby boomer approach were now seeing them from a different point of view. One executive started the conversation regarding weaknesses in their managers, which led to a conversation lasting over half an hour and ending with his comment: "They are the weakest link in the organization which was exposed throughout this year. They have, in fact, increased the risk to our organization through the crisis, as they have lost much of our knowledge through the necessary head count cost cuts."

Further frustrations expressed were that sales managers were limited in their responses to the market and to management requests for change and growth. The executives observed that some sales managers have continued to hold organizations at ransom with the mantra of "I am central to success approach and without me you will lose the last remaining customers you have."

This is a very dominating approach that can instill fear in even the most experienced executives. Those executives have lost more revenue and asset value in just the last year of 2009 than over the equivalent accumulative five years prior. The thought of further losses is a major concern to them with end-of-year report looming.

Some sales managers have elected to exit the market and seek other careers as executives rejected the "we will lose all the customers if I go" approach and started to ask more invasive questions regarding performance than previously asked at meetings. Some have been exited from the business and replaced, as they could not articulate the way forward or answer the questions, or generally exhibited attitudes and behaviors that directors no longer accepted.

Like the customer relationships that disintegrated under pressure, the loyalty to the sales managers has disintegrated with the pressure of the new world that organizations are required to operate in. Long-term relationships with employees are now faced with the difficult conversations, advising them that the end of their career with the organization had arrived. Other executives unable to face the decision of termination with long-standing employees, are seeking alternatives in how to address their organizational problems.

The other point that also needs to be considered is that these sales managers are the mentors and most experienced salespeople in the market. They have created the next generation of potential sales managers.

There is a growing divide in this next generation, as some have remained exposed to the limited experiences of working with one or two employers and limited sales management while others have sought further education and gained degrees in business and other disciplines. Those with different employer experiences and business degrees have exposed them to a different set of standards of business requirements than have been applied to the sales organization in the past.

When the past will not manage the future

For the first time in history, a major challenge has arisen for salespeople as organizations demand more structure and process applied to sales organizations and the sales organization management is not equipped or sufficiently developed to embrace the change. The salespeople are being required to comply with organization requirements with little support from their managers. They are operating in a twilight zone. Often sales forces are blamed for non-performance, but on closer analysis they have been hindered by being asked to operate in this older-style methodology and lacked the support and processes they needed to excel.

This is something that I see more often than not, and companies are suffering unnecessarily.

We are now seeing Generation X (30–45-year-olds) moving into higher-level management roles and the difference in management styles has become more evident. Gen Xers are less trusting than their baby boomer counterparts and certainly expect a more transient employment record. There is a mix of those who are Internet savvy and willing to document performance and those who are not. Those that are educated in business degrees and those that are reliant on skills gained from being mentored by the previous managers are more open to learning a more disciplined sales process and following structures, but they feel confronted by the need to report their performance, whether in sales roles or management roles.

Another impacting point is the CEOs they report to. Often the CEOs hold skill sets that provide them with only the historical view of how sales organizations should be managed. It is not part of their tenure to be intimately up-to-date with modern sales force requirements, and they are reliant on the sales managers to bring to them current and relevant processes. As like CEOs expect from their production, logistics, and other areas of the business. Regrettably, many sales organizations are lagging well behind the adoption of new methodology and best practice against other departmental areas of organizations.

Most Generation Xers, as managers, take a less trusting approach than their predecessors, as they are well aware of their own conduct as salespeople and know the loopholes and traps they were able to step around with their own managers. They intuitively know that salespeople need a more careful eye placed over them to ensure they are performing the tasks required in the role. They are more attuned to hearing both sides of the communication—the real information and the hidden information. They are less likely to accept being held at ransom by sales individuals who will not divulge information on customers or build barriers between the customer and the organization. They are aware of the lack of value of many of the management reports previously attempted to be used and in particular the call report, but very few actually implement reporting structures that give the transparency required to effectively manage a team. They still have a strong tendency to operate autonomously and look for salespeople that operate in autonomous environments.

They face a unique challenge as they are in the middle group of people that are either pulled toward the baby boomer style or into a new set of demands rising from their team members. The result is dependent on the business profile and age of the salespeople. Some industries attract age groups of the Gen X as salespeople while others see the emergence of the Gen Y into their ranks.

As the oldest members of Gen Y (20–29–year-olds) take up sales and marketing roles, their expectations of resources and support are significantly different from those of their predecessors. They have been raised in an Internet environment and consider instant communication, reporting, and process to be part of life. They are keen users of technology and willing to operate within structure. They are from the learning generation and expect to be developed consistently in their roles. These salespeople are demanding of their managers as they seek guidance and coaching and are very quick to question any directives. Their questioning is not a defiant trait. They are merely a generation that seeks understanding before engaging in a task. They follow what they understand and do not just blindly follow any instructions provided to them. To this end they require more in-depth conversations and thought applied to any directive; the more complex the directive, the more likely it is that questions will arise. They seek consistency in management and consistency in the communication to them. They seek feedback on their efforts with far greater detail than that most managers are accustomed to providing.

For the sales managers that are exposed to this generation through families, it is less likely to be a shock to them; but for those that have not had the exposure it can seem very confrontational and uninviting to hire, let alone manage, on a day-to-day basis.

Many organizations struggle in their sales organizations (and we can imagine that other areas of the businesses are equally challenged) to meet the demands of these individuals. This demand, however, is not going to disappear and companies have to learn to work cohesively with them.

I was speaking with an international sales manager recently discussing some internal challenges he was experiencing.

Some regions had more mature salespeople and they had three regions that were all Gen Y salespeople. The sales manager was challenged in managing them as he could not understand their short attention span. He found he had to coach and guide them every day to keep them focused or they quickly strayed away from the tasks they needed to complete. He was shocked at the amount of follow-up that needed to be done to ensure proposals were lodged timely. As a group of regional sales managers, they had all debated various ways of managing the situation and the resulting conclusion was that they needed daily management. They also found that even after months and in some cases after up to a year in the team, the same process had to be applied. Gen Y's ability to complete tasks timely and stay focused was their greatest challenge to managers. The time invested was considerably higher than what they have had to apply in the past.

The cut-off point for sales managers

Sales managers are now faced with the inevitable task of needing to change their beliefs and behaviors in how they will operate in their roles. Their acceptance of accountability, responsibility, and transparency will be minimum requirements for gaining and sustaining employment. The art of sales will be replaced once and for all by the science of sales management.

Sales managers have to expect rapid change in how they operate themselves and seek outside assistance to identify the required changes so they can deliver a razor sharp strategy implementation with their teams. They need to move beyond just thinking about customers and relationships and engage with all the areas of true sales force effectiveness and ensure the sales organizations are correctly balanced in all areas to deliver the required outcomes in the short, medium, and long term.

Sales managers that excel in the future are the ones that raise the bar on themselves and their teams, creating highly competitive sales forces in the new markets. They step-up to challenge, embracing change in themselves and effective leadership of their teams.

Chapter 5:

Shifting to Excellence in Sales Organizations

If the need for change is identified, then now the question becomes: what degree of change or transformation do the executives need from their sales organizations? Too little is demotivating to the team and the organization as a whole, as the effort reaps no real rewards. Too much can destroy the fabric of a company, as the change is overcooked and too much unnecessary disturbance occurs in the business.

I remember a company I was working with in Chicago that had embarked on a transformation program several years ago (pre crisis) and decided to change the fundamental way in which the sales organization was managed. The focus was placed on the salespeople and attempting to create a performance culture with a technical sales force. The concept was correct; however, they had instigated changes that the company was not prepared for, and within six months the entire business was destabilized. The culture of the business had developed to such an extent there was no trust between the team and the leaders, as the team felt they were victims of performance management with insufficient tools to support them. With realignment of all the right ingredients and the emphasis placed equally back to how the team was managed and performance guided, the company rebalanced itself again within four months.

I have seen many attempts at change where insufficient effort was applied or simple solutions were sought. Too often, managers were just looking at the compensation plans as the key to future. If it only it was that simple!

What is the measure for 'how much change'

As I often convey to people within sales teams, if you want to improve your personal performance by 10 percent in sales, you will need to make a 20 percent change in what you are doing. Fundamentally, change will only occur where crucial change to processes is applied. For a salesperson, just changing your objection-handling skills or closing tactics is not enough.

You need to audit your entire sales effort from sales planning and customer segmentation through to actual selling capability. Only then do you achieve sufficient change that will be sustainable in the short, medium, and long term.

The same degree of change can be applied to sales organizations, but you need to step back and look at the broader aspect of everything that affects the sales organization. Change can be a very positive thing for organizations, particularly when sales forces see the relevance of the change to their future. If you are raising the bar and creating a highly professional environment, you are more likely to succeed than if you are just focusing on performance.

While many organizations are now applying world-class standards to manufacturing, logistics, financial, and operational areas of their businesses, their sales organizations seem to have been left well behind. Sales forces are renowned for not being accepting of change, and often the person required to deliver the change is the highest resister—the sale manager.

One of the washouts of the global financial crisis is what it has exposed inside companies how they operate. The crisis has demonstrated the depth, or lack thereof, of management that has been applied to the sales organization in the past. When sales forces were reduced in size and asked for changed behaviors in their sales efforts and changing customer bases, many CEOs were very concerned over what remained. More importantly, they feared all the knowledge and history that walked out the door in the heads of former employees. The company had lost valuable resources that many other companies had already instigated processes to protect.

The laissez-faire leadership had taken its toll on sales organizations.

Lessons learned

Chief executive officers and chief financial officers (CFOs) are beginning to demand greater accountability from and control over this previously mystical area of a business. They are drawing on lessons learned in other areas of the business and applying that same practicality in how they expect the sales managers to respond.

They are seeking more transparency and sales managers who can manage not just the human component of their teams and customer relationships. They require a person that can manage all the risks associated with customers, employees, knowledge, process, measurement, and all other contributing factors while bringing about market alignment. They are seeking a businessperson rather than a now-dated, narrow profile of a people and relationship manager.

The role of the sales manager continues to mature as organizational demands increase and performance comes under more scrutiny. Many clients report to me that the sales organization is the last frontier of formalizing their business processes. They have worked through all the other areas and when they reach the sales organization they have already established high standards across their business. This can further magnify the problems they see in the sales organization.

Often clients report that during executive meetings they find the responses from sales managers to be repetitive and lacking business acumen. The sales managers seem to focus on negatives rather than bringing sound solutions to the table and action plans for implementation. Interestingly, in the Harvard Business Review research into the behavioral traits of sales organizations, they identified that some 66 percent of sales organizations failed to operate with consistent systems and processes that would ensure their competitiveness in the market.

Is a world-class team really relevant?

For change to occur successfully, you need to pinpoint what level of change you want to achieve. More importantly, you need to accurately define what you are going to change the organization to and how it will operate in the future. When I am keynote speaking with executive audiences, I often ask them if they wish to be world-class; interestingly, some respond that they don't feel being world-class is relevant to them as they only deal on a local level. I inquire if they source product or materials from outside the local area and they respond that they do. They produce products to world-class standards as they have to compete on a stage where products from other regions and companies are presented to their customers.

After a few moments, the penny drops and they realize that if their products need to be world-class to compete, then the sales organizations goes hand in hand with that standard too.

The reference to a "world-class" level is often spoken of as a generic term, but it is important to understand exactly what the term implies.

1. World-class means having a clear picture of success. It is very specific, measurable, and results oriented. It is not based on effort alone.

2. World-class means focusing on the things you can control. Pinpoint the things you know you can improve upon that are totally within your control.

3. World-class means avoiding excuses. If you rely on excuses, they will always surface when the going gets tough.

4. World-class means consistently performing at top levels. It is not a snapshot experience based on one achievement. In fact, world-class today will not be world-class tomorrow because the bar keeps rising.

5. World-class means believing in breakthroughs. Success does not have to be a methodical step-by-step process with only incremental improvements. World-class performers prepare for quantum leaps in performance improvement.

When we consider the effects that world-class standards will have through a sales organization, you can immediately feel the tension that will be experienced within an organization as it broaches the subject with sales management. The difference in behavior from where many are operating today to where they need to be tomorrow is significant; my experience is that it is rarely met with the applause and open arms of joy.

This point brings to my mind Dr. Spencer Johnson's cultural change book, Who Moved My Cheese? If you have not read it, jump online and order a copy. It will save many hours of debate and discussion. It will also give perspective to the following statement.

The writing is on the wall

Many sales managers and senior executives are now at the crossroads where they will begin to see the writing on the wall and the necessity of adapting to change. The long tail of the crisis has given rise to the need for change and the permanency that is required for new methods being adopted. For those that don't see the writing on the wall, it will be a hard road ahead when finally the realization arrives.

Organizations need to make the decision over which direction or road they will be taking. The road to the right being paved with potential and the road to the left being paved with more of the same. They are at the crossroads where the decision will define how the organization will compete in the future and its sustainability in the changing markets.

For some organizations the change will be catastrophic and affect the organizations as a whole. The way the sales teams have been viewed and communicated with across the organization, and the way the rest of the organization has interacted with them, may need to change completely. For other organizations it will mean making adjustments and alignments to absorb the new processes as the companies have already begun the journey of organizational integration. In either situation change is inevitable, and the sooner it is started the better the experience for the sales force and the organization as a whole. The change is about aligning to the market and improving the effectiveness and competitiveness of the company.

What I can advise you is that the change will not just affect the sales organization if it is to meet the standards of today's marketplace; the tentacles of change will wander into all corners of the organization. Those that implement change without impact across the organization are actually not making sufficient change for the overall success of the desired outcomes.

Sales managers are faced now with being change leaders—an extremely hard role to fulfill when they are going through personal change themselves. Typically, they have not experienced what the business should be like and are unfamiliar with many of the ingredients and orders of implementation that are required.

This does not mean they cannot embark on change, but certainly they need a well-proven and scripted method to follow so they can focus on the right things in the right order to achieve the outcomes.

This is often a major barrier to sales managers taking the steps toward change or the unknown. There are very few places you can go to learn this in a timely manner and a limited number of people that have worked at those standards and understand the journey required to take a sales organization through to that level. Change reluctance is a fear in every person, and sales manager's fear is being wrong or losing credibility in front of their teams. They often stand frozen in time, knowing they cannot go back and cannot move forward. They do not wish to seek guidance from within the organization, believing the company expects them to know what to do. They see it as a point of weakness to admit there are elements that they are unsure of, uncertain of the team response and certainly uncertain about changing their existing beliefs in such a transparent and raw method.

Laying down the path ahead

Interestingly, once you lay down the road map in front of sales managers and set out exactly what is required, I find they are motivated through the fear barrier and successfully lead change programs with their teams. The knowledge of exactly what to do and the sequence of actions is the confidence they need to move forward.

Getting ego out of the way

I was working with a team of sales managers based out of Wisconsin, with decentralized teams across the United States segmented through product divisions. Each of the managers was successful in his/her own right and had delivered good results for a sustained period of time. The CEO was looking to raise the bar with the team and increase its knowledge base to a more commercial focus with more business practices adopted in how the teams were managed.

The initial resistance from one of the sales managers was intense, with every subject challenged and debated rigorously. The constant statement was, "we are already successful so why should we change?" The ego was bigger than life itself and the mind was closed tight.

With support from the CEO between sessions, we saw a change in attitude start to occur, with one or two of the managers starting to implement just minor points they were learning and getting successes with their teams. The change started to escalate until finally the person that was the least supportive became the most supportive of all the new methods and disciplines being learned. Their individual implementation processes were proving successful and the results started to lift with the team.

Fortunately the CEO had made the decision for change at a time when change was not really a priority but he was dedicated to staff development. When the crisis arrived at their door, they firstly had all the right information to make sound decisions as it happened. Secondly they were able to deliver growth in the business units during a collapsing market. Those sales managers are now operating at an elite standard, providing excellent leadership to their teams and business management to their units.

The key to their success, and everyone's, is being able to focus on the right points to change, in the right sequence to create the best outcome for the teams and organization.

With the inevitable need to change to a more structured and disciplined approach to the sales organization, the question arises as to what that structure will be and how will it be shaped within an organization. Commonly the structure and discipline are about creating more transparency and not looking beyond this point to what else is available to the sales organization.

When simplicity is a tripping point

There have been attempts made by organizations to structure sales organizations in the past, and many seek simplistic tools to assist them in the quest for more transparency. The two most popular ones adopted are sales process improvement and installation of the CRM. These are seen as central to the improvement of any sales force. If you can teach salespeople to sell better and record their activities in a CRM then you have everything you need to excel. The CRM will manage opportunities and ensure they sell enough with their new selling skills from sales training.

If life were simple, there would not be a dysfunctional organization in the world today.

Vendors and consultants communicating these simplistic approaches often have a narrow understanding of business and fail to understand the full ramification of change management and business requirements. Typically I find when speaking to the sales trainers that they are average sellers that have gained access to a well-branded sales program that they teach to teams like they are reading out of a prayer book. They may be entertaining and inspiring at the time, but many have no idea of the impact of their statements across a company. They have very little commercial acumen. The CRM vendors, again often representing a major brand name, are of similar ilk.

Implementation of these two points will bring you up to only the most basic level and not to a competitive level. These are the most basic of points to address that any company can take and often are very poorly implemented and followed through on.

In a recent article from one of the major CRM magazines (name withheld purposefully), they reported that the reason most CRM implementations fail is that the systems are too complex to use. Users were unable to effectively access and operate CRM systems across various devices. They then went on to say there were some systems available that were simpler to use with easier access. This is not only a simple summation of why CRM uptake commonly fails, but probably a marketing ploy from companies that sponsored the article indirectly.

What my experience has demonstrated is that the reason most CRM implementations fail is broader and often embedded more in the culture of the business than the software itself. There is also an overriding issue related to the age group and beliefs of those in management. If you reflect back to the previous chapter, you will see the obvious correlations between successful and unsuccessful implementations impacted by age and leadership styles. We will discuss this further in the book in chapter 13.

The disconnect between senior executives and sales

In an extensive research program in 2009, my consulting firm, Sales Focus International, reviewed over eight hundred sales managers against organizational demands to develop a clear view of the potential disconnection between the CEO, the CFO, and sales managers.

Clearly, in the past, senior executives of organizations reported their complacencies in challenging improvements in this significant profit area of businesses, often not knowing how or where to start remedying the problems. They were more willing to look at product improvement and software, as these are inanimate subjects to discuss, than to look at issues surrounding human capital and how teams are managed. Most executives were resigned to the fact that sales was a different world within their organizations—one they best left alone and that was stimulated through incentives and new products. While some performance was being achieved through this stimulation, it still does not address many of the business requirements for a sound organization.

Senior executives reported that they saw sales organizations as an area of characters—great communicators whose primary focus was to maintain connection with customers. As they did not follow any demonstrable business process and produced no business reports to speak of, they were generally considered to be a relatively immature and unmanageable area of the organization. Their tasks were customer satisfaction/loyalty and repeat business, with some new customers where possible.

This low expectation often prevailed in organizations that had matured to a point where the business had gained its own momentum in the market and that momentum could be retained with little input by the sales organization; or in situations where the organization was riding a wave of strong demand for its products. Marketing, not the sales organization, was often seen as the major contributor to growth. Growth was gained through repeat business and new product releases, but not by taking market share by the sales organization. Market share was gained through organizational acquisitions and mergers.

The smaller organizations typically felt that the turmoil associated with the sales department was just the turmoil of business. They had no points of measure that business could be different and they relied heavily on the caricatures of the sales managers to be their lynch pins in the market. They felt the business would suffer significantly without the larger-than-life personalities that the customers seemed to be drawn to (according to the sales force).

As discussed earlier in the book, with the experience of the global financial crisis, CEOs and CFOs are changing their expectations of sales managers. No longer do they accept the cowboy approach (lone rider under laissez-faire leadership) or that of the motivational king that creates hype among the team; instead they are looking deeply into the sales managers' business acumen and ability to operate within a well-managed, disciplined environment that both protects brand image and drives growth.

These business leaders are seeking hard evidence that the sales business unit is being managed effectively to maximize profit through internal and external cost control. They seek knowledge management, risk management, and all the other elements that are common to other business units.

Many senior executives have described their greatest challenge as being able to find the individuals that have matured their skill levels to such an extent that they can be seen as serious contributors at C-level business meetings.

For many companies, that quest to find a suitable candidate is not going to be realized, as the number available in the market versus the number of companies seeking them is well out of balance. Those that are capable of managing sales organizations at those levels are demanding premium incomes and only work in companies where all the right ingredients and overall cultures are in place for them to excel in their roles. They have the pick of the market.

The rest of the companies need to develop suitable people through their resources and ensure the longevity of those people in their employ. For sales managers this presents an enormous opportunity for skill improvement and development of a sound career for the future.

Chapter 6:

So What Are You Actually Aiming For?

The measure of success can be debated by all executives and depending on the journey your business has taken, that success can be seen through many different eyes. One of the primary debates I have with entrepreneurs is, "successful compared to what?" I remember this debate in particular with a gentleman quite a few years ago who had built an international company, a strong brand—and what he had achieved was remarkable. The debate was a joyful conversation with him as I challenged (smiling) whether he could be more successful. After he let go of the history and our conversation moved to the future, he agreed the business could sustain rapid growth as it had all the right ingredients in place. His mindset moved from applauding success to date, to focusing on success to be achieved. Sales doubled in the next three years, year on year.

To be successful you have to establish a benchmark of what success will actually be and what you are striving for. That will be your success that satisfies you but may not satisfy others around you. Some may say it's too big as a goal and others too small. It is what you want.

The vehicles you take to market will define how difficult that journey will be, and the people in your team can provide you with opportunity or may even cap your growth. The people of an organization define its success, as they are the living element that put into action all the requirements of the business.

In sales, the sales manager will be the defining person. He or she will define the quality of the people in the sales organization and how successful the company is in the market. Great products do not guarantee your success. Great people do.

Sales managers, like all management positions, have fluctuating skills and experience that will define the level of value they deliver to businesses. The key is to understand more clearly what those skills and experience firstly are, and more importantly what they need to be.

Sales Focus International research studied the full gamut of sales management—from first-line manager through the person who has earned the right to be titled chief sales officer (CSO), capable of contributing significant value to the organization.

It is like finding a needle in a hay stack

The CSO is a rare individual, commonly found in a larger organization where structures have allowed this person to escalate in his or her role– organizations with the resources to develop the role to such an extent that the person was taken in through an apprenticeship of excellence over a number of years. The apprenticeship is one of formal education, training, and mentoring outside of the sales organization; and, importantly, it requires the resources to apply the business requirements within the sales organization. This individual cooperates seamlessly with the marketing department to ensure that all growth strategies are translated into hard money results.

Those hired in smaller organizations are challenged by lack of funds, by the day-to-day pressures of being under-resourced and, most of all, by roles where taking the step toward a more strategic function is hindered by cumbersome and often dated business functions and requirements. Many have opted for a verbal-management-only approach as it maintains their tenure with the organization and ensures job security. They see this as a point of survival within a hectic environment—an environment in which they live day-to-day, month-to-month. Forecasting is based on gut feeling and trust in the sales individuals to bring in the revenue.

These sales managers are often capped in their careers. CEO/CFOs have often failed to understand the overall impact that investments of business improvement could deliver to their businesses. The sales managers neither seek education to improve their situations and the business processes nor do the CEO/CFOs demand it of them. The CEO/CFOs are comfortable with the sales managers' primary focus on production and operational issues. They see sales as a task of customer care and relationships. They are commonly advocates of the Pareto Principle, being the 80/20 rule where 80 percent of your business comes from 20 percent of your customer. This principle allows for operational predictability and cost control.

For the CEO/CFO to hire a sales manager that changes the dynamics or places upward pressure on the executive is seen as disruptive and problematic to the overall business, as the executives have not learned how to manage or respond to what a sales organization with world-class excellence would be like. Very little exposure to such organizations is available for smaller businesses, and many training vendors are unable to provide sufficient knowledge to enable them to learn. In fact, they train in the old models of sales management which are now redundant.

In Sales Focus International's review of organizational demands and generational skill, some strong trends emerged. The research found that, where the skill of the incumbent sales manager was lower than actual organizational requirements and others in the organization needed to have further input into the process to compensate for the problem, often the reduced cost of hiring the lower-skilled incumbent incurred a much higher cost to the organization as others took up the missing elements of the role. Where the organization and generational delivery failed to meet, there was a considerable impediment to the organization's ability to grow. There was a high level of lost opportunity for new customers and within existing customers. The gap between the organizational demand and the delivery capability usually fell at the point where more planning and analysis were required to exploit all the opportunities available to the business.

It is all a big misunderstanding

In our analysis of requirements within an organization, an interesting, yet expected, trend appeared.

Many of the words associated with organizational demands were common to the marketplace, but there was a distinct difference in the quality of performance that surrounded them. Many references lacked sufficient depth within each section to be effective and deliver the value of outcomes.

A simple example is the process of defining territories by drawing lines on a map—in contrast with actual analysis of potential target customers, mix of audience, potential revenues, and allocation of territory based on projected revenues and geographical. The first approach shows the greatest exposure to lost opportunity and high cost of service; the second approach ensured that all opportunities were secured at lowest cost.

We often find that people will quickly scan over all the points in the survey and place a tick against each of the functions. What they fail to do is examine the depth of application and interlinking between each functional activity within the sales organization.

I recently experienced this with an international trading company that had developed a number of systems and processes internally. The company was successful but wanted to drive sales revenue higher. On conducting an audit of their business, they produced a number of items that were part of their sales processes and procedures. Conceptually they had the items and would tick the boxes on the checklist, but on inspection this is what was found:

1. A sales training program that was from IT sales background being applied to selling capital equipment. The program was also some ten years out-of-date to current market selling practices and had many important gaps that would be costing them high-value dollar sales

2. A pipeline report that was incorrectly aligned to the business requirements and was providing only about 10 percent of its real value to the business

3. Sales reporting that failed to deliver measureable performance indicators

4. Duplication of processes between sales reporting and CRM

5. A CRM system that operated at bare minimum information and failed to support marketing and sales integration

6. Compensation plan failing to support business requirements

7. Sales meeting formats that added no value to salespeople

8. And the list goes on.

This company is not unusual and we have audited many companies that have suffered from the same situation. Most have taken a few ideas from past employers and tried to dovetail them into new businesses. The systems are disjointed and not specific, and they create more work for everyone than outcomes.

The absolute truth about sales managers' capabilities

On reading the generational requirements and sales force effectiveness requirements, please reflect on them considering the depth you have in place rather than relating to the subheadings alone.

In the research, across the board, Sales Focus International was able to identify six specific generations of sales management. Larger organizations often retained several levels within their structure while smaller organizations unfortunately often struggled to work with under skilled people at the early stage levels.

First Generation

These sales managers typically have Baby Boomer attitudes, whereby the business is conducted on trust and verbal communication. Their business processes are focused on motivation, reward programs and interaction between one individual and another. They are strong promoters of relationships and the importance of the connection between customer and salesperson, rather than customer and organization. No business process is applied to the identification of human capital requirements. They commonly have a higher cost of sale.

Individuals in the team are prized for their product knowledge or industry experience and, therefore, attract high levels of salary in compensation for bringing that knowledge to their organizations. They make small changes that have interim effects or no effects on the overall sales capability of the organizations. They surround themselves with experienced individuals who require a lower level of management and input into their performance.

Organizations are exposed to the rise and fall in the markets in which they trade. Growth is typically organic and actions are focused on matching competitors.

Primary Traits of First Generation Management:

- Customer targeting

- Sales meetings or gatherings on an ad hoc basis

- Individual or team budgets

- Basic compensation plans

- Promotion of autonomy

- Product sellers with little consultative selling capability

- Verbal team reporting

- Performance measured on basis of historical figures

- Team autonomy

Hiring criteria for team members: industry experience, strong seller, likeability, customer connections.

Second Generation

These managers have taken a step forward from the first generation in their pursuit of management of the individuals within the team. However, the established culture often limits their ability to progress. There is a sporadic use of documentation but a lack of consistent focus; therefore, the results reflect the wavering focus.

Primary Traits of Second Generation Management:

- Territory management strategies showing immaturity

- Account management strategies showing immaturity

- Performance reviews given annually

- Individual budgets with under budget performance acceptance

- Sales training with irregular timing

- Individual coaching on an ad hoc basis

- CRM system with low take-up within team

- Product sellers with a consultative approach

Hiring criteria for team members: industry experience, strong seller, likeability, customer base, sales training and CRM exposure optional.

The first and second generations are the most populated area of sales with 78 percent of sales managers being in these generations.

Within this grouping, 34 percent reported that they would not adopt any changes to their practices.

Third Generation

The sales manager in this generation is often found in an organization that has achieved some degree of size and maturity in the market. It will have grown to the point where it can invest in the sales organization. The organization will have developed stronger HR management skills, which they naturally gain benefit from. There will be more focus on sales team activities but there will be little follow-through in initiatives and implementation of new processes. Typically the sales manager will be drawn to focusing on the top 10/20/30 customers or customers with significant value to the organization. There will be little development of new customers as the focus remains on nurturing existing customers.

Primary Traits of Third Generation Management

- HR systems—organization-wide, not specific to sales organization

- Early stage, activity-based management

- Simple knowledge management/sharing

- Distribution engagement strategies

- CRM system with low to medium uptake, where some team members are not engaging at all

- Maturing account management strategies

- Maturing territory management strategies

Hiring criteria for team members: industry experience, strong seller, work within structure, consultative selling capability, professional training, territory management capability.

Fourth Generation

Often at this stage the sales organizations will be well populated. National managers are in place with regional manager reporting lines. They are well educated and experienced across the broader business demands and, therefore, understand the impact of decisions made in the sales departments across the organizations. They have strong focuses on market intelligence and understand the impact of cross-functional systems and policy, minimizing the impact of the sales organization on other areas of the business. They make most of the hard decisions in a timely way. There is evidence of early stages of work-flow control to increase productivity within the business.

Primary Traits of Fourth Generation Management:

- Sales planning

- Human capital planning

- Cost control of sales head count

- Knowledge management

- Sales cost control

- Risk management—human capital

- Risk management—financial

- CRM system—high uptake implementation

- Sales compensation and rewards aligned to corporate goals

- Cross-organizational efficiency

- Performance reviews quarterly

- Brand management—human capital

- Analytical and strong follow-through on tasks

- Quarterly performance reviews

- Leadership based on set goals and requirements within team

- Role clarity

- Strong induction and educators

- No individual greater than the business in knowledge

- Lead tracking systems

- Defined selling practices

Hiring criteria for team members: degree qualified, strong seller, work within structure, consultative selling capability and professional training, territory management capability, sales channel experience rather than industry experience. Able to learn new products rapidly and technical resources used to advantage with customers.

Fifth Generation

This generation has many of the traits seen in the previous generation but applies considerably more business acumen to the management process. These sales managers are approaching the level of fully competent Sixth Generation chief sales officers.

Primary Traits of Fifth Generation Management:

- Processes of Fourth Generation

- Sales channel and distribution

- Cost to market

- Marketing communication

- Marketing intelligence

- Brand management—collateral

- Budgeting based on capacity planning not historical

- Sales efficiencies on internal sales resourcing and reducing costs

- Tracking salespeople across at least fifteen metrics weekly

- Integration between sales and marketing ensure consistent communication to the market

- Brand management of individuals and collateral

Hiring criteria for team members: capable of operating at level four, as they are commonly national managers with regional management reporting to them.

Sixth Generation

This generation is the matured chief sales officer who sits alongside the other C-Level executives and makes a significant contribution to the business's overall strategy. These sales managers often have level-four managers reporting to them and they are well-informed about the businesses and how to drive the results.

Primary Traits of Sixth Generation Management

- Translation of strategic plans in detail

- Market research—structured and reliable

- Pricing

- Product mix

- Contributions to strategic management based on research facts

Although there are instances where some actions are not taken by individuals from higher generational levels, the core of their efforts define the team performance where their efforts are applied.

When one considers these identified generations, the impact of their performance on an organization's success is clear and the ideal person to hire is Fourth Generation or higher.

However, there are very few such CSOs operating in the market. As noted earlier in the book, the key is to hire them and educate them to the business's requirements, ensuring that appropriate business structures and resources are available to progress them in their roles. It must be a project within their roles.

Often in smaller organizations the CEO takes on the role unknowingly of CSO and employs a frontline sales manager who is required to perform limited tasks.

The biggest challenge for organizations is that many sales managers are in the first or second generation—some through choice and others through the exposure of the companies they have worked for. The question is: who will have the attitude, motivation, and necessary behavioral traits to be educated to the fourth generation and beyond?

If we look at the pressure being experienced by organizations in a survey by Sales Focus International in third quarter of 2009, the following trends appeared:

- 82 percent of marketing strategies that were greater than twelve months old were failing to meet market demands in changing environments.

- Only 23 percent of respondents said they had reached Harvard Universities' classification of Level 3 (of 4 levels). Harvard's classification of level 3 being those who typically enforce use of a standard process, but typically look backwards and, therefore, are constantly missing opportunities in changing markets.

- Only 11 percent of respondents said they had reached Harvard Universities' classification of Level 4. Level 4 being those organizations which dynamically monitor and provide feedback on sales force through the use of systems and process to ensure best-practice productivity and effectiveness. These organizations can detect even minor changes in the market and respond. These organizations are formidable competitors and achieve the highest levels of growth and profitability.

Note: The Harvard Research is outlined further throughout the book.

To the questions about the most common approaches to performance improvement, we received these responses:

- Does CRM improve sales and marketing performance? Only 22 percent of respondents said it had made some difference to their organizations and many were still greatly disappointed in the results being delivered. Many communicated their concerns regarding the cultural impact following the commencement of implementation. Under 9 percent reported it had made a significant impact on their businesses.

- Will sales training alone improve sales performance? Under 5 percent of people reported a sustainable increase in sales.

When you review the research of generations of sales managers, there will be many different responses to it. Some will say their businesses are different (a common response). Some will say it is not necessary for their industries. Others will see value in building the sales organizations, and a small group will already be on the path to success and looking to further formalize what they are doing.

The great cover-up

Often the senior executive or directors will cover up for the missing skills by believing they can nurture the sales manager with their strategic prowess, leadership, and competitive product, releasing the sales manager to focus only on the day-to-day team requirements. They basically have the sales manager operating as a field manager or team leader with a larger title, which fails to respect the positive impact that quality sales management can have on an organization. It also lowers the professionalism of the organization in the market, as customers have the opportunity of more comparison of other sales managers from other vendors, whether competitive or not.

A nurtured sales manager is often unaware of the impact of his or her decisions at field level and unable to identify when opportunities and specific management techniques are required to ensure that the organization excels.

Nurturing sales managers also creates a lower level of accountability, which flows through to the sales force.

The manager's salespeople are a direct result of how they have been guided and managed. In fact, after 120 days, they are a direct reflection of the manager. When the sales manager is lacking in specific skills, this has a significant impact throughout the sales force. If there is no intervention or major change made, then the manager will define where the team is going in the future.

As noted earlier, the road to the right is paved with opportunity, professionalism, and growth. It's a difficult road insofar as it requires dedicated drivers and there is the need to navigate numerous twists and turns. A sales manager does not necessarily have to have passed the test prior to heading down the road, but certainly the manager has to know when to stop and ask for directions. And those directions need to come from highly competent people in sales organization effectiveness and not just glorified trainers of the sales process with a few templates.

Chapter 7:
Working Out Who Will Drive the Bus

Sales managers across the world have now reached a crossroad in their careers. To the left is a career that is based on more of the past, and to the right is the road to new skills and methods and longevity of career. The question on the signboard at the crossroad is, "Who wants change?" Only an individual can make that decision. No matter how much coaching, nurturing, debating, and even pushing you give someone, it is his or her personal decision about what he or she wants to do. That person is either 100 percent committed or not. Someone who is just 90 percent committed is in reality not committed at all—they are still looking for the door that will allow them to escape the change.

There will always be a place for all sales managers—those that make the change and those that don't. Why? Because they will work for CEOs that too are required to make changes or elect to follow past practices. Those that elect not to change are the businesses that do stand the higher risk of failure through lost profits, market share, and other factors, but they will be around for while now if they have survived the financial crisis.

Sitting at the crossroads

Crises in business and life often bring about the most likelihood of change. There has been sufficient time for organizations to analyze what happened over the past few years and set the new strategy moving forward. They now need to look at who will be instrumental in driving the business forward into the future.

After some twenty-plus years of consulting in transformation for sales organizations, this would be considered undoubtedly the most optimum time I have seen and one where the most amount of discussion is occurring in how the sales organization will be shaped in the future. I have also observed the impact of change being attempted when everyone is not committed and organizations are full of passive-aggressive individuals— those people that agree but never take any action.

I have seen the results of organizations that were tentative but committed to change and the outcomes delivered for them and their teams.

Sales managers need to make the decisions and this book may assist in shedding some light on what degree of change you personally need to make if you wish to operate a world-class sales force that is highly competitive.

If you are a sales manager or aspiring to be one, as you read through the research throughout this book, you will see the enormous opportunity that is being placed at your feet. The financial crisis has brought to the forefront the time when organizations will make significant steps forward in their business models, and sales organizations will be central to those changes.

This is the time you can break tradition and change the upward trajectory of your career as a sales manager or business manager. You are in a position for rapid improvement in the current market, as all the ingredients are there now for being a catalyst for change.

You can bring about the change within the sales organization that may well put you down in history within your organization. It is a time to show initiative and desire to adopt new methods, no matter how difficult the change will be.

Sales forces are also at a point where they are most likely to accept change, as they are looking for ways that will assist them in the field. They are looking for leadership, guidance, and assistance that will remove the barriers for securing sales. They seek smarter business models that will enable them to do their jobs more effectively as they will have the right information to make decisions at the customer interface.

Sounding a little "rah rah"? Well so it should. It is a rare event when senior executives are faced with a major dilemma of taking the left or right road with their sales organizations. It takes a crisis in the organization for them to stop and reconsider the core of how they do business and how to move forward in the future. They have had the crisis; it was a global crisis, not an exclusive one.

Senior executives are not as shy about being seen to be impacted by a crisis as they would have been just four years ago when everyone else seemed to be doing fine. It's simply what is happening to many organizations now. Organizations are looking for a way out of the dark and a way to manage the risk so they never go back there again. They are looking deeper into their organizations for answers. They are looking for people that will step up and seriously start playing a new game.

They understand that the skill demands have changed for sales managers and that rapid change is required now for real-time results to be achieved. They are not expecting sales managers to arrive one morning with new skills but they are expecting them to take action to put the sales organization in the right direction. Senior executives are now more open to that sales managers being coached and/or guided to deliver the changes. They actually expect this to happen to ensure success for everyone within their organizations.

CEOs are open, if not demanding, to implement processes and systems that will give the transparency and accountability without the criticism and cynicism of the past for the information surfacing through the transparency process. They are looking for improvement and taking a positive view to improving on their current positions.

It is a defining moment in time

Clearly the organizations that will excel in the future are those that take the steps now to create new sales cultures within and a new leadership style and set of priorities in how teams will be managed. They will be led by people either capable of or striving to be fourth-generation-plus leaders (referencing Sales Focus International research documented earlier in this book). Those sales mangers striving to be fourth generation will be people that are dedicated to achieving new sales cultures and leadership in reasonable commercial timelines of fewer than twelve months followed by sustainability.

The sales managers leading the change will be people who are not entrenched in processes from the past and skeptical of the future. They will be open-minded and embrace the opportunity to drive the changes. They will enjoy a little of the unknown.

They will desire to develop business acumen equal to their sales knowledge, will be able to learn, and will understand the full ramifications of their role. They will embrace the role of educator and leader of the sales team members, taking them on the journey to the new sales culture.

The organization will set new benchmarks of the minimum performance standards in the business. It will set the bar high so it is competitive in the future, not just catching up to where others are already operating. The new culture is benchmarked not against its original culture but against world best practices.

Choosing the right benchmarks

Why do you need to benchmark against world best practices rather than personal best or organization best? Personal or organization best will yield a measurable increase in your own internal performance, but this level of increase will not be a measurable level from a customer's perspective. At all times the measurement must be against the customer's experience and not your industry experience.

Organizations often fail to acknowledge that customers gather their experience from other businesses selling to them and not just in direct dealings with their traditional vendors, from their office supplies through to large capital expenditure items—anything that has involved a salesperson's interaction to make the purchase.

Those vendors can be either local or global organizations bringing potentially unprecedented levels of expertise to your customer. Given this, your competitors are potentially the least of your concerns. Your customer's experiences with other vendors are your greatest concern. An organization that is used to purchasing from sophisticated and professional sales personnel backed by highly efficient sales organizations is not going to gain respect for the lone autonomous seller of yesteryear. Your whole industry could be similar in how it operates; however, that does not guarantee you will get the sale. You may well find your customer heading offshore where they can find the level of professionalism they are used to dealing with. Your lack of ability to respond to them at the desired level as a sales organization may also lead to failing to meet their expectations and potential conflict in the relationship between both organizations.

You also need to consider how advanced each person from the customer organization is in his/her own sales organization as, in fact, you're competing against that as well. Their experience will set the expectation for your organization.

High-performance teams are led by high-performance managers in well-structured and disciplined environments. When you consider some of the successful sales organizations, they have managed every element of the brand, from marketing material to sales representation. People know how to be effective in their roles, what processes they need to apply, and what behaviors and performance deliver the required outcomes. There is a high level of transparency and an environment of learning and development and not criticism. They operate as the collective intelligence rather than being led by an individual. The strategy of the organization is translated to the market in a seamless process with the results of overachievement.

Changing times-changing people

The times have changed. Not that long ago, sales managers were being ostracized for being different. Those managers capable of delivering the results were often quickly removed if their behavior was seen as different from how the organization had done business in the past. The new sales managers rocked the status quo and salespeople revolted quickly, knowing they had the ears of the executives. Regrettably for the organization, but fortunately for the individual, those talented individuals left their employment and often started their own organization.

There are two types of people: those that can make the change and excel, and those that talk about the change and fail (for any reason other than their own performance).

I remember a few years ago being exposed to an organization related to the financial markets. It had one of the most exceptional salespeople I have had the privilege to work with. He was disciplined and very astute in recognizing opportunities. He had previously held a role of sales manager in an organization and had excelled in the role. He was making a strategic move from his previous industry into the financial market area in his career where we found him.

His sales manager was, at best, a poor salesman and the executives had obviously modeled themselves on Gordon Gekko from the movie Wall Street. The business was in trouble. Even though this one salesperson was bringing in more revenue than all the others combined, he was never accepted as one of the team because he was different.

After completing his apprenticeship in the new industry, the salesperson resigned and opened his own business in the financial markets. Within one year he had squashed his previous employer to a poor operation in the market; within two years his business was recognized as the leading provider of those services within the financial markets. Interestingly, he survived the global financial crisis with flying colors and continues to build his business to even greater heights.

You sure you don't want that person in your organization because he's different???

The moral of this story is: just because people are different does not mean they are wrong. They may well be showing you the way forward, if you are only willing to get on the road with them. Clearly they are experienced and have been thoroughly reviewed for their experience. Their actions are based on measured performance. The key is to have a measure on what should be installed as best practice to validate the actions that are occurring. That is good risk management for any organization.

Heading out west

Another type of manager I've seen a lot (in fact, too many times) is the one who wants to take the business into unknown and often unproven territory. These managers are often perceived by the executive as high risk, but the claims they make give the executives the confidence to take the risk. They achieve the first major sale for the company, being that they sold the senior executive on their abilities. The managers have often been hired before the strategies, knowledge, systems, and processes are installed, as organizations believe they will be installed by the new incumbents.

Everything is verbal. That is the first sign of trouble. Often these managers talk about a desire to make changes. They expend considerable time building the vision of the future, but no structure, discipline, or process is put in place.

There may be some token gesture items but nothing that provides a base line or foundation that is required for effective sales organizations.

They are motivated by making statements to please weary audiences of senior executives and those less-skilled senior executives in sales organization who fall prey to their great communication skills. They make promises about systems to be implemented, changes to be made, and anything else that senior executives want to hear.

At each milestone, there is little to show and no apparent change. Each of these managers is just another person through the management cycle and a replacement is soon found. Interestingly, the executives often hire another manager who promises changes and conveys the intention of putting in systems. And the cycle starts all over again.

Fact or Fiction

If an organization is looking to hire a sales manager that talks about implementation of systems and processes, it should drill down further and find out exactly what those items will be. There should be a timeline established of when each element will be installed and measurement against best-practice requirements. If the intention is actionable the person should be hired.

If you have a sales manager that states an intention to implement systems and processes and to seek external assistance, then they too should be hired, as their intention is actionable.

If anything was learned from our research, it was that many of these managers reliant on verbal management failed to install anything—not even the basics that would support growth. Most opted for the simplistic approach of a CRM, demonstrating their own lack of knowledge in performance improvement.

Often these people were demoted quickly with the uneasy feeling of relinquishing control without an understanding of where the business was changing, how it was changing, and what the long-term effects of those changes by the senior executive would be. The other frustration was the length of time it took them to complete tasks.

Even after six months, there was little evidence of any change. The world moved on without leaving your organization behind.

Some quick investigation would uncover that they had never operated within the environments they said they would install. It was conceptual to them and conveyed as a selling tactic during hiring. The problem is that most senior executives have also not been exposed to high performance environments therefore they are unsure what they are evaluating against. External sales transformation (not recruiters) expertise can be justified very quickly when such high-level placements are being made.

These experiences are all going to impact the decisions of hiring of sales managers in the future. Organizations will be open to the person that seems different but wary of the person that does not have a disciplined approach to how they will bring about the change. Executives will want to see hard evidence of what changes will be made and how those changes will be implemented. They will be more than wary of the person that does not provide the documentation for the changes to be implemented, as it will be a red warning flag to the "gift of gab" person from past experiences.

The sales manager that presents himself or herself to the senior executive with a structured approach that can be project managed through the business is the person that will be respected and well paid. Whether that person is currently hired, an internal promotion, or an external new hire, he or she will be on the top of the list. The person will demonstrate where the skills have been learned or who he or she will be engaging to assist the sales manager through the process.

Interestingly, when production managers are looking at improving their production capabilities, they engage external expertise to assist in guiding them through the process. We have seen that a lot in lean manufacturing and other operational expertise areas.

Sales managers see it as a weakness to engage external expertise, and they attempt to make improvements on their own. They operate in a trial-and-error environment with the highest risk possible to the organization. Their failures can have major and long-term impacts on the companies' top-line revenue and overall sales culture.

Sales managers from Gen X are more likely to engage with external expertise than those of the baby boomer era. Gen Xers have come from an era where learning is part of a management role, where baby boomers are those that believe they have to have all the answers—a good consideration to include when you are hiring a sales manager for your sales organization.

Senior executives realize more than ever that the people capable of bringing about the change and transformation are not lone rangers or heroes that save the day. They are not people that are verbal operators by nature and demonstrate no structure in their own conduct.

They are actually people who are skilled in identification of issues, selection of the right resources of knowledge and experience to implement the changes, and the ability to manage the project to completion. They are good project managers as well as people managers.

They are people that are sensitive to the timing of transformation in a sales team and understand that it cannot be delivered effectively over a longer period of time. The sales organization typically tolerates six to twelve months to succeed in a transformation.

Over the past few years I have witnessed an extraordinary number of former sales managers and executives enter the consulting market, conveying their prowess as people who can change sales organizations (and other area of the business). They extol their own knowledge in leadership and other non-tangible aspects of business management. Companies have been inundated with offers of consulting services that will change their lives forever. In fact if you look at when they started consulting, most were around 2008–2009. Coincidental? I think not. These are the first cut of people that were exited from sales organizations for nonperformance or the business being exposed to high levels of risk and unable to perform in changing markets.

There has been a major shift in how consultants are hired and certainly they are now viewed more from a candidacy perspective than from the perspective of the consultant with a great offer. I had an interesting experience in late 2010 when a US company approached me to undertake some work with its sales organization.

The company revenues were around $100 million per annum (post crisis) with a large decentralized sales force. They wanted to transform the sales organization to a world-class competitive sales organization. During the meeting the CEO announced that I would be required to complete a psychometric and executive competency test. Taken aback momentarily by the requirement and thinking my track record would speak volumes, I agreed that would not be a problem. After negotiating the commercial terms and everything was agreed, the testing went ahead. The organization was operated by a very astute CEO who understood the impact of good and bad people on an organization. He was also weary of consultants not delivering over the past years and understood the impact the assignment could have. Fortunately for me I scored in the top 95th percentile of executive management with a major US leadership evaluation company.

It was a significant point in time for me and changed my view and standards for consultants for the future. When you consider the damage that has occurred from inexperienced consultants over the years, in all aspects of business services, executives have to draw a line. They need to be sure that who they are engaging, the team members within a consulting firm that will work on their account, are best in class. A reference from a friend or a good pitch just no longer cuts it in the new era of services post the financial crisis.

You are engaging services of individuals that must be able to deliver significant results and raise the overall standards in the company and not just deliver mediocre outcomes. To be world-class you need to take quantum leaps forward to ensure you are highly competitive in the future.

Who's driving the bus

The same measures need to be applied for sales managers. Are they capable of delivering a transformation and adapting to new markets? If you tested them today would they have the abilities to deliver or do you need to educate them? Do they have the core competencies required? Are you attempting to take a highflying top seller full of ego and selfishness to be a person who is inspired and motivated to deliver results through others?

Does the sales manager really want to be a sales manager or just see it as a way to get out of selling or as the next step in his or her career, without understanding the full requirements of the role?

The person that will fulfill the role within the organization must be carefully selected or reviewed and in most cases a sound development plan put in place. You are most unlikely to pick one off the shelf. Whoever is the person that ends up driving the bus (your sales organization) will be pivotal to the future success.

Chapter 8:

Why Some Companies Take Unnecessary Big Risks

In an earlier chapter I mentioned that sales managers and executives have reached the crossroads where they can take the road to the right of change or the road to the left that is more of the past. It would be remiss of me to provide some insight on just the right road that needs to be taken, without giving some insight into those that elect to take the road to the left.

It is all about security and status quo

The left road is not as glamorous and forward thinking and is more related to safety, due to insecurity about change or lack of desire-identified need to change. It is the road that follows along traditions of the past and pursues incremental changes, if any at all. It is the road of complacency or security for senior executives that believe they have only minor issues to address and they are fundamentally a sound and profitable (if only minuscule profit) company. The left road is one that attempts to nurture the lack of skills in the sales manager, who often does not demonstrate any desire to change. Often the person coaching the sales manager is the CEO, who feels he or she is making a great contribution to the person's career by providing the coaching. Fundamentally the sales manager does not want change and has shifted to being a passive-aggressive profile, listening to the CEO out of respect and the fact the CEO pays his/her salary.

Interestingly, this road keeps sales managers contained in smaller role requirements so they are easier to manage. The focus is just on people management and customer management. These are organizations that dislike confrontation with their personnel and seek stability, and I often hear the reference to being a family or similar terminology. Time is never an issue for them and they just like to go about doing things quietly in their own time. They dislike any employees that will potentially rock the boat. They rarely seek external opinions and if they do, they are often not acted on. These companies are risk averse and see any form of change as a risk.

Interestingly, although this is the road followed by those who are risk averse, they do not realize they are actually taking the biggest risk of all.

After many years of consulting, it is difficult for me to understand why people take this path, but then I do have the advantage of being very experienced in what it is like to be at the other end of the road. Typically the companies taking this direction have not had the exposure to top performing teams and really don't know what positive impacts it could have on their sales organizations.

Focusing on the lowest denominator

What we know from experience is that many times an organization makes the decision to continue with the existing manager when change is inevitable, and invests its time in nurturing the sales manager's attitude in a hope that this person will change. This is done through a combination of both the organization's loyalty to that person and its security in staying with someone it knows.

What it fails to realize is the message that is being sent to the team and others in the organization as the business goes into a holding pattern while it deals with the way the manager operates. The decision must be respected, but also balanced against the impact across the organization.

Often the manager is blocking progress in the organization with no desire to change, feeling that the changes will expose him or her as ineffective. There is then a major shift at the executive level as it becomes a mission for senior executives to not be seen as failures in guiding the person as they attempt to change the manager. They think they can mollycoddle the manager into change and that the manager just needs time to adjust.

Senior executives need to examine their motives for not changing and examine if those answers are really supporting the overall development of all the individuals in the business and the security of the company in the longer term. Are they fixated on one individual rather than all the individuals in the business?

Tough decisions have to be made in tough markets. Decisions need to be made to ensure the security of everyone in the company in the future.

My line is always that individuals make their own decisions as to whether they want to embark on transforming an organization. If the CEO does not want change then it is the end of the subject. If the CEO wants change but there is individual resistance after initial education, then that person made the decision for you. If their attitude is good but their skills are poor, they can be educated. If their skills are good but their attitude is poor, they have also made a decision.

Another fundamental point is that no one individual can be greater than the business. This means that you cannot put the business on hold for one individual to come around to what are commercial requirements for the operation of the business. You can allow a certain amount of time but then it crosses a line into being a barrier to success rather than an adjustment period.

Cash flow dries up patience

I would suspect that in the future there will be less tolerance of the poor or passive-aggressive attitude that blocks change, since organizations do not have the financial resources to support the large costs to their businesses of slow change. In the past, many companies have expended large sums of money trying to ease people around to new ways of thinking. They believe change takes one-two or three years. Those timelines are totally unrealistic in today's world for sales organizations.

For those that are unaware of the term, passive-aggressive people will seem to be accepting of change and will give you the right answers to every question. The only noticeable thing is they never seem to follow through and make changes. They are very good at shielding themselves from being identified by focusing your attention on others. They can be found sitting the closest to the strongest power broker in the organization, as they are focused on politics and getting through the change unscathed and unchanged. Ideally, they want improved status in the organization without any effort applied. Promotion by association! The inexperienced change consultant or manager often thinks the passive-aggressive person is the greatest ally in driving the change process, only to find that he or she has been ousted as a consultant and that the passive-aggressive person has risen to the top at his or her expense.

Often we find that senior executives taking the left road will make several attempts at change and then finally one day their patience runs out. It can be the simplest of things that tips the scales in the opposite direction—a statement in a meeting that is the final straw or a well-favored customer lost to competitors.

Should a vacancy become available following an attitudinal issue with the last incumbent, the next person will bear the brunt of those actions that retained the person for an extended period of time. The sales organization has learned how to debunk people from the company or who to turn seek support from and keep things at the status quo.

The same mistake over and over again

Often senior executives immediately head straight into the recruitment process without giving thought to the changing needs of their businesses. They try to fill vacancies quickly rather than consider what is really required for the businesses. Often they hire similar types of people as they hired in the past and get very nervous because of the different people they meet. They want more of the same but with better attitudes.

If they are strong advocates of industry experience and relationships, they will hire people with those qualifications, forgetting the other fifty-odd requirements they need. Certainly the people will not bring about sufficient change as they also reliant on industry and relationships as their primary skill base.

The recruitment organizations may not be as advanced as they should be on this subject of sales organization excellence and are often motivated by the commissions and wanting to fill the vacancies quickly—particularly in markets where vacancies are limited. Recruiters are not going to say, "Let's stop and give you time to reengineer the sales organization processes and prepare it for the new hire"--not the ones I have dealt with anyway. They want to fill the vacancies as quickly as possible and often present senior executives with a stream of the "gift of gab" managers that promise the world, while remaining completely unaware of what they are presenting.

The managers' resumes have the right industry background and they are good communicators. For some less-talented recruiters, this seems to be enough to qualify for presentation to the organization. Those organizations that have longer-term relationships with recruiters will definitely get better service where they understand their clients' business drivers and requirements.

For most, the recruiters will still promote the old adage of relationships and industry experience as they fail often within their own organizations to have any form of structure and process to their sales organizations. They know their clients will feel a degree of comfort with candidates from that background and with the perceived ability to bring customers with them, thereby filling the vacancies quickly. Why complicate what can be a simple placement?

If the senior executive incorrectly hires a new sales manager, the outcome is well documented in this book already.

Growing your own

If they elect to move to an internal hire (which may also be for head-count restrictions in this current climate), regrettably many organizations, when recruiting internally, do not take advantage of times for change and prepare their businesses with strategies, knowledge, systems, and processes that support the promotion and ensure everyone's success. The change of leaders can be an optimum time to introduce change and project manage the processes into the business. Such an approach would certainly be a sound risk management for organizations serious about growth.

Many companies are now at that turning point when past performance will indicate future performance due to the lack of change in the hiring process. It will definitely depend on the position description documented, but most will be hiring on pleasant conversations and good intent; it is a sad fact of life.

So what actually occurs when you recruit internally and do not take the opportunity to develop the business processes? The best way to explain this is to tell the story through an actual client experience, one I have witnessed on many occasions throughout my consulting career.

Many readers will relate to the following story, including those who have fallen victim to such a scenario and those who have had to clean up the mess afterward. Senior executives will reflect on the story and wonder why—when it's so obvious—it actually describes what happened to them.

A generous promotion by the director—with consequences

Peter, the director of the family organization, promoted Bill internally to the role of sales manager. Bill had a solid track record of fifteen years' experience in the organization in a few different departments. He had started work with the organization fresh from school. His background and experience centered on selling. Peter and his family felt comfortable with Bill and felt the promotion would cause the least aggravation to the existing team. Bill was certainly a personable man who was well liked by the customers and all those working in the organization. Bill was a natural promotion as he had demonstrated some leadership qualities by assisting others within the team.

In his new role Bill immediately focused on spending time with the team, always available to assist them and certainly adopting an open-door policy. The business continued without disruption and overall the promotion was a popular move for the executive. There were no repercussions for them and no pressure placed upon them by a new person coming into the role.

Over the following few years, the organization continued to prosper and customer retention was excellent. There were signs of profitability diminishing, but this certainly was not attributed to the sales force, as they were not directly responsible for the profit. The profit was being lost through increased customer demands in the form of delivery timelines and product requirements, which were affecting production. Meanwhile the sales team regularly visited their customer base and was excellent in servicing requirements.

In Bill's fourth year of management, things started to change. A new competitor had entered the market earlier and was now starting to take market share away from Peter's organization. Customers were still ordering but the average order value was falling and the frequency was falling.

Peter looked to Bill to take action to offset the competitor behavior and Bill immediately advised the team to increase their calls to customers and spend more time with them. He encouraged his team to service customers vigorously and meet any customer demands, so no further losses would be incurred.

Profitability continued to diminish as the cost of service increased. Peter again turned to Bill to take action to offset the diminishing gross revenue and profitability of the organization. Bill turned to his team and asked them to start finding new customers. His message this time was to focus on new customers. He indicated that customers who were over demanding may have to be replaced. The team started making some new customers calls, but was unable to bring the business over to Peter's organization. Bill organized for the team to be trained to brush up their skills, but there was still no impact on the gross revenues, and profits were continuing to decline.

Peter was now faced with a management dilemma. Bill was a long-term employee and certainly there were strong loyalties to him. Bill clearly was unable to perform and the organization was starting to seriously suffer from the financial impact of the changing market. The lackluster results were lowering motivation across the organization as employees became increasingly aware of the problems. The sales team was respected for its product knowledge and therefore had to be retained to ensure that the customer base was not further eroded. Peter's board of management was pressuring Bill for a change of management to bring about growth again.

After a period of time, Peter was faced with having to recruit a new sales manager who could bring new methods and ideas to the business. He discussed the situation with Bill and it was agreed that this was best for the business at this time and that Bill would confine his role to looking after the key accounts. It was an amiable situation that everyone could work with.

Peter went about recruiting a new manager and found Stanley, who had a track record that would add value to the organization. Over a twelve-month period, Stanley worked hard to bring about the changes required and develop some new practices in the sales force. The sales force was reluctant to adopt any changes and often sought counseling with Bill.

Stanley attempted several different methods of creating change and when he approached the subject of replacing the team members, Peter was quick to block the thought, as he had confidence in these team members. Stanley threw in the towel and left their employ.

After twelve months, very little had changed in Peter's view and he turned to Bill and asked him to take over the team again. Peter communicated to the board that Bill was a quality person and the need for a change back was further evidenced by the lack of performance from the new manager, who had now departed. The team was pleased to have Bill back as the sales manager: he understood them better than Stanley had and things quickly settled back to the way they were. A couple of Stanley's ideas were kept but most of them were considered not really appropriate for their industry.

Peter was convinced that they needed new products, not changes within the sales force. He set about developing new products and believed they would expand the business in the hands of his loyal team who had stuck with him through all the turbulence of the last twelve months. The organization continued to struggle with profitability and it was advised that it was just how the market was now. Peter told himself that times had changed and he would just have to live with it.

What happened here was that Bill had not developed the skills and expertise to effectively manage the team. Educating Bill over the years was not a priority of the organization, as he had been an internal promotion and their loyalty to him blinded their ability to see his weaknesses. They placed little value in the role of the sales manager and, therefore, assumed no new skills were required.

It was like an old marriage. Everyone got along and had the occasional little confrontation but all in all things just ticked along. Bill understood the business and knew how things were done, so it was considered that giving him training in sales management could add little value. He was an industry and product expert, which was far more important in their view of the world.

The business had developed its own processes and methods over time, which had created its sales culture reliant on people and their longevity of employment. The employees and management had little exposure to professional sales forces and believed their way of doing things was how the entire industry operated. They were product focused and believed great product would save any situation.

With the changing marketplace, those traditional processes and that sales culture were being tested, yet the market changes went undetected for some time because the organization did not have in place the tools needed to recognize the changes when they first appeared. When Bill was asked to respond to the changing markets, he did not have the knowledge or experience to do so. When you consider that was a small change in the market compared to the global financial crisis, then you can safely assume the organization may have taken a turn for the worst.

The incoming manager walked into a long-established culture. Any form of change, no matter how incremental, would have required intensive management to bring about the behavioral changes that could have delivered results. The manager would have spent most of his time trying to effect behavioral change within the team, so any meager results would fail to address, let alone outstrip, the marketplace changes.

So what is down the left road?

In summary for this chapter, when senior executives take the left road, they really need to seek outside opinion as to whether they are doing it out of a desire for comfort, a lack of knowledge, or an inability to confront the tough issues. There are many quality and highly experienced advisors at the senior leadership level to assist you in gaining a quality analysis of whether the senior executives are prepared and desirous of change. This needs to be analyzed before engaging with the sales organization levels. The sales organization will not change if the senior executives are not fully engaged with the requirement for change and what that change will be and mean to them.

Clearly, my advice would be not take the road to the left, as it's paved with loss of profit and high risk disguised in temporary comfort of the known.

Chapter 9:

Looking at It from a Sales Manager's Perspective

To date we have looked at sales force transformation from predominately an executive point of view but we really need to see what is ahead for sales managers. Is this all doom and gloom or is there opportunity here to be seized?

There will be one of two scenarios that you as a sales manager will be in at this time. One, you may be applying for a new role, which gives you an enormous opportunity to state your case and demonstrate your talent, as you start from a neutral point and ideally an unencumbered point. Two, you may be an existing manager within an organization who has decided it is time to make the changes and lead the organization to a new level of success.

That latter is a harder task to complete, as the people you will be selling your transformation project to have already drawn opinions of you and have in mind where you fit in their organization. If they see you as a leader of change and improvement, you will have an easy task ahead of you. If they see you as part of the sales team with a title for larger accounts, it will take more effort, as you have to change their opinions to sell the project.

If you are stepping up to the role of sales manager from within the team or another team, people may be open-minded to listen to what you say and what you can demonstrate. If you take the ego approach of saying you have all the answers, this will be received as high risk to executives. If you approach this as a well-managed project using expert resources, sales force transformation will present with credibility.

What is the best-sized organization to engage in transformations?

There is also the challenge in the size of the organization you work with that you need to be aware of.

Larger organizations look for people who have done apprenticeships through the business and gained the knowledge and experience (both academically and in the field) to hold the position.

Larger organizations operate through process, as it is the only way they can manage large groups of people; therefore, the common functions that are required for all personnel, not just salespeople, are already in place. These include support services such as training managers, HR managers, and systems management, all of which contribute to how the organization is operated. In larger organizations, sales managers are limited to being people and customer managers and complying with established systems. A transformation project requires many sponsors and contributors to get off the ground and make it to completion. The cultures in large organizations are often prohibitive to change based on the lack of sponsors.

Rarely do you see in corporate business a person go from salesperson to chief sales officer with major leaps over the apprenticeship steps. You will see this person move through the ranks of sales individual, team leader, sales manager, regional sales manager, national sales manager, and then chief sales officer. If you reflect on the information chapter 6 on the generations of sales managers, you will see this career development is comparative to the fourth, fifth, and sixth generations, depending on the advancement of the large organization.

If you are working through those ranks there are things you can implement within your area of responsibility that will place you in line for the promotions as they arise. You need to have a set of tools, disciplines, and processes that demonstrate you are standing out from the pack and maximizing the performance of your team. Senior executives are commonly seeking organic growth and profitability to meet share holder returns. Organic growth being defined here as being the growth of the company through its internal resources, rather than through mergers and acquisitions.

In midsize organizations the hiring process is less sophisticated, and often you will see people move from sales manager to national sales manager with little change in their role. Internal promotion of unskilled individuals is a common action of small and midsize organizations.

Often the sales manager is reporting to a chief executive officer, who is the primary contributor to the strategic direction of the organization and the requirements of the sales organization. With the CEO playing this role, he or she is removing some of the senior tasks typically associated with the sales manager position. In these organizations you have the greatest impact on the businesses, as they have grown large enough to understand the need for accountability and responsibility through systems and process, but are not mature enough that they have sealed off their minds to change and improvement. They are commonly driven by senior executives with entrepreneurial spirits that seek growth well above industry levels.

The small organization has typically not matured and is limited by the talent of the managing director. It is interesting to note that small and midsize is not dictated by annual revenue. It is the number of employees and maturity of the business. I have seen many midsize companies of revenues fifty to one-hundred million that are behaving like small businesses turning over ten million behind the façade.

If you work or intend to work for a small business, you need to ensure that the CEO is an adopter of best practices in business and open to change. If so, you have an outstanding opportunity to excel and prepare your career to move up to the midsize organization. If the managing director is a person who seeks comfort and no risk, then you will be managed by the people around you and change will be a difficult task. Your decision is regarding whether you can educate the managing director or whether the effort will take so long it will not be worth the outcome.

I have seen situations many times in smaller companies where managing directors will limit or cap the growth of their businesses purely as they will not relinquish control once the businesses reach a certain size. They have a set of behaviors and beliefs of how they like their businesses, and even in the face of great growth they subconsciously sabotage their businesses.

Capping growth CEO-style

A few years ago, one of our Sales Focus International (SFI) consultants was working with an organization that had capped its growth at twelve million dollars.

The managing director was a shareholder and been in the role for ten years. The board had identified the sales problem and engaged SFI to resolve it. Our consultant delivered a 40 percent increase in sales in six months with sustainable processes in place. It was a job well done until the next couple of review meetings were conducted. The managing director was able to pull the business back faster than the consultant could grow it. He had agreed to a set of tasks and stated he was doing those tasks, but he was subconsciously pulling the business back to his own comfort level.

The consultants went back in again on request from the board and turned the sales back up by 25 percent. More counseling meetings were set up to assist the managing director through the process and to ensure that changes were achieved. We elected to use an independent consultant for that task of counseling and sadly they reported back to us: there was no change and the business had been wound back again.

Finally the board saw the writing on the wall and changed the managing director. The business doubled in size over the next three years.

All sales management roles have their challenges. The key is to make sure the organization has what it takes to support and achieve business-process improvement, changed behaviors, and sales performance.

Who will get the role of sales manager in the new marketplace?

With the value of hindsight, the hiring process in the future will have a different set of values and attitudes than seen over the previous ten years. If you review the job boards, you will see the two different styles of advertising now occurring. One is asking for someone with a strong network and relationships; if you continue to read, you will see these organizations are looking for saviors that will bring customers with them when they are hired. These are the desperate companies looking for lifelines. They are caught in the past, working hard within their businesses, and have not stepped back to see what is needed for the future.

The other type of advertising is the one asking for strong coaching skills and new customer development skills. Sales managers must be able to implement systems and processes to effectively manage the team. These companies have digested what has happened and decided the past will not be the future.

Their hiring criteria have changed to meet the new marketplace. They are looking for one of those less available sales managers in the market today: the ones who can deliver in the new world.

Those companies that are seeking to create world-class sales organizations with a strong focus on profit and commercial conduct will have a different attitude and perspective into candidates' resumes. The hiring criterion of the past has become the barrier for many to the future. We have put together some insights into how those executives are reviewing candidates.

- The sales manager with twenty years' experience in one industry may not be seen as an asset, but rather as a liability: a blinkered person who cannot adapt to the outside world.

- The sales manager who produced great results in the past (pre crisis) is no longer recognized as a person that excels. Companies want today's people that have delivered through the crisis.

- The sales manager who creates hype and focuses on motivation as the primary form of management is seen as a dinosaur, much like those that believe in laissez-faire management regimes.

- The sales manager incapable of providing effective and well-prepared sales plans and strategies is considered to be no more than a glorified salesperson.

- The sales manager who is considered for promotion from within the company, will only become a candidate if they have worked through a career path and been educated in modern practices that can challenge and drive the business forward. This person will receive all the necessary support as long as he or she has made the first step of getting educated (regardless of who pays for the education).

- The young, enthusiastic salesperson who communicates that he or she can do a better job than the incumbent is now seen as a high-risk person who must have extensive systems in place to manage effectively.

- The sales manager who is averse to transparency, accountability, and responsibility is seen as an underperformer. This person will have to have demonstrated these skills and not just give verbal support to them.

- The sales manager with limited IT skills or understanding of business practices across all divisions will no longer be carried by other managers or directors.

If your resume and conversation contain any of the traits that are no longer in favor, then you need to rethink your approach and potentially work to learn and demonstrate the required skills of today.

The candidates that will be well regarded are those who:

- demonstrate the understanding and skills to develop marketing initiatives to break new ground and grow existing customers. They must be sales-force savvy and have strong customer development skills.

- has the ability to be able to combat competitor activity without resorting to price. They must be strong, added-value sellers or business case sellers in their own right and capable of coaching salespeople in skills for all customer situations.

- demonstrate their business acumen is balanced equally with management-leadership skills and selling skills. The higher the position (CSO), the less emphasis on selling skills as the role evolves to business management and commercial prowess.

- will have operated in fully transparent, highly systemized environments where best practice is fundamental to how a sales organization is operated.

Smart companies apply more stringent recruitment practices

Executives are far more cautious now in the recruitment process, and skill testing and psychometric testing are standardized in the process even more.

Executives will be looking for more depth in discussion of how a person will develop the business and transform the team to world-class standards. What behaviors you will install in the team and how you will drive the profitable growth will be most important.

The other factor that will be a defining element hiring will be the timelines that people will be expected to deliver the outcomes. That is something everyone needs to bear in mind.

Sales managers who will succeed and be paid handsomely are those who implement world-class sales organizations, as everyone associated profits.

Sales managers must keep abreast of the subtlest of changes in the market to succeed. Opportunities present themselves in fleeting moments in the market and will not remain for long with the current high level of competitiveness. The problems that take away customer spending will move rapidly through a customer base, and competitors will be working hard to aggravate problems in the eyes of customers in an attempt to win new customers. Sales people will be presenting sound business cases and reasons for the customer to change suppliers (if the competitors' teams are being correctly managed too).

Through the global financial crisis, organizations are internally and financially bare and many have battled to stay in business. The focus is now on growth and development of new sales cultures that will support them into the future. To accept that responsibility and deliver on it will be the key to a sales manager being prized in the market.

When existing customers are considered high risk

For many sales organizations, the security blanket of the existing customer base was whisked away from them as those customers failed to survive in the changing in the market. Sales individuals that focused purely on existing accounts were tortured as they watched their customer base diminish before them.

In 2009 I spoke with a man in Toronto, Canada, who said his role was to manage twenty major accounts for his organization. On the topic of new customers, he said that was not part of his charter and a skill he did not really possess.

He was a specialist in major account management and nurturing the relationships and growing those existing accounts.

I asked him his strategy for account protection now that the market was more active with desperate competitors. He said that the longevity of the relationship and intimate knowledge of customers' business would hold off any attack. He was convinced of it.

I then approached the subject of risk management, asking about his strategy for managing the risk of his customer's downsizing and reducing the need for his organization's services. He agreed there would be some downsizing but said that new products would take up that gap.

I rang him not long afterward to follow up and find out about his progress through the financial crisis. Canada was a late entrant into the crisis and he had not felt the full effect when we first spoke. He was already in a distressed state, however, as his customer base had collapsed by 47 percent in just a few months and he had no way of recovering the losses. I asked him if he would look at new customers to manage the gap and he confirmed that the only way to recover was to continue nurturing those existing accounts and hope they would come back with the market recovery.

People can be very fixed in their views and not see the writing on the wall when it is obvious what the future will hold. This man was steeped in tradition and the sales culture of existing customers and had no connection with new customers. His selling approach was overly trained in customer management and devoid of the skills required for finding new customers.

The organization ran the dated approach of hunter/farmer, a business practice that was in my opinion always an excuse for poor performers. What it actually meant was that farmers (the weaker of the sellers) were left to look after the farm and stave off the attacks of the hunter, a highly efficient seller capable of winning at all costs. That's like leaving the kids at home to stave off the thieves. This sales culture is rampant across many organizations. The larger the organization, the more likely that this culture will be in place.

Two consistent traits of problem businesses

Interestingly over the years of completing many reviews and turnarounds, a couple of consistent points that appeared in companies with problems were (a) hunter/farmer methods being applied to sales force structure, and (b) the 80/20 rule on the customer base. They are practices that close minds to opportunity and not really open them. It may be that they are not applied correctly in the business but then it begs the question, why did so many get it wrong?

Opening the door of success

There are many great opportunities for sales managers in the new markets if they have the right mindsets and are willing to learn new skills and methodologies.

Many sales managers will be taking on roles in the future that will be problematic due to the past practices of the companies. They will need to be driving new markets, and they will experience new pressures, new competitors, and new ways of doing business. They will need to keep their minds active and alert and have the ability to seize opportunities with their teams as they arise. They will need to be trusted leaders in the entire process—the people who are the leaders, the guiders, and who are capable of managing the necessary transformations within the sales organizations. They will be smart at hiring specific resources to assist them and not cap the businesses potentially by being the only knowledge contributor.

A person that acts timely and seeks support where necessary to ensure the business achieves it goals will be the successful manager. They will act in such a way that their egos will not be blocking sound business decisions.

Executives that have broader expectations of the sales manager as being more than a people and customer manager will provide great platforms for success for all those involved.

Chapter 10:

All You Ever Hear about Is Systems - We Are in Sales!

Over the years I have engaged in many discussions regarding systems, and everyone agrees they are a necessity in operating a business. However, most people relate systems to processes applied to finance, production, and human resources departments, and when it comes to sales there is a major gap in the business. What any business advisors will tell you is that it is absolutely critical to the future growth and success of your business to have systems.

Why? Well, systems are essential for

- building the asset that will generate the greatest return on investment (ROI) should the business be sold;

- creating the order and structure that will produce your intended outcomes;

- producing consistent, reliable results each time, every time, with minimal indirect costs.

Even before you intentionally set out to systematize your business, you'll probably find there are some systems in place and functioning in your business right now. For the sales organization, most of those systems are verbal communication on how to get things done.

If you think more about it, everything that gets done in a business is done by following a system of some sort. These may not be effective systems, they may not be consistent, they may not be written down, but a good number of systems are already there. One might say that most businesses function with systems that exist by design or by default.

Systems that put you on the moneymaking line

With sales organizations, I often speak with business executives about the "moneymaking line."

A series of actions with the right focus and degree of consistency produce the desired outcomes of revenue and profitability. If you step off that moneymaking line by just say, 5 percent, then you are losing revenue either in the top line or the bottom line, or both.

Having the right systems

This was best highlighted at an organization that I reviewed a few years back that was looking to raise the overall performance of the business. The company was successful, delivering profit to shareholders, and operated in a fairly systemized environment. The company was a manufacturer and was going through the process of introducing lean principles in its production area and was well on the way with that initiative. The concept and value of systems was not new to them.

The sales organization was a typical business with some twenty-plus salespeople in the field, all reporting back to head office. They were a mix of ages and backgrounds and the company had a low turnover of staff. The sales manager was engaged with his team and quite an organized sort of person. On first meeting with the executive team and the sales manager, the business was one that you would immediately get the feeling from that this is a well-run business. The sales manager was apprehensive of the review occurring but was respectful of his CEO and agreed for it to go ahead.

The focus of the review was to confirm the elements they were doing correctly and identify areas of improvement so they could achieve additional revenue.

As I worked my way around the business and looked at the physical systems in place, they were all fairly rudimentary and served their purposes. I then attended a sales meeting and had the opportunity to speak with some of the salespeople. They were nice people and the company had done well in hiring them. They respected their sales manager and had confidence in his ability to lead them.

The next step was to start drilling deeper into the business and look more closely at how people went about their roles on a day-to-day basis and review the functionality within the teams.

What I found was inconsistency within a number of areas that would take the business well off the moneymaking line. It would still produce revenue but nowhere near what it was capable of delivering. The business operated on the typical interpretations of what needed to be done rather than providing absolute clarity of what needed to be done. There was a lack of attention to detail in the sales-planning processes at all levels, which allowed for varying degrees of going off the moneymaking line.

I put the business through a series of analysis processes that identified how much revenue it was missing and where it needed to refine the business further. I presented the findings to the executive team and sales manager and they were surprised over how much revenue could be gained with improvement in the systems. We then provided the sales manager with a working project guideline for him to implement, which he accepted readily. (He received performance bonuses and could see the benefit to himself, his team, and the company.)

The outcome: 25 percent increase in top-line revenue and an additional four points of net profit on the bottom line in twelve months.

So the question of "Should you systemize?" could actually be reworded as "Are you dedicated to profit and asset value?" The executive may be more motivated about that than some employees, but that is the reason you are in business: increased profit and asset value.

Often, when the matter of systems is raised in conversation with executives, they immediately look to the financial reporting within the organization. They can run a plethora of reports on customers by product, turnover, and margin, and then this can be extrapolated to regions and a myriad of other reports by design. With the onset of more advanced ERP systems, it means the reporting capabilities on products and financials is endless.

In asking for more details on systems, some organizations extend the approach even further to systems that relate to quality assurance: the process to be used when entering orders to the financial or operational systems, and the process to be used for credit notes and other compliance obligations for the effective operation of the organization.

Risk management demands systems

As indicated throughout this book and validated in the research, there has been a strong tendency within organizations to operate sales forces based on people's knowledge and longevity—not only within the business, but within the industry—notwithstanding that this long-held knowledge is not actually recorded anywhere (allegedly because there is too much of it to document).

Knowledgeable, long-term sales personnel have been traditionally perceived as making high-value contributions and ones that must be respected and retained. Executives and sales managers feel comfortable with a person who is deemed to be the industry expert, with many years of nurtured relationships he or she can draw on to support the sales effort. It is an easy cushion for sales managers to allow these individuals to operate freely in the market, bring in sales results, and be at times moved to legend status within the organization. The individuals themselves very comfortable with a free lifestyle, no reporting, and going their own way every day.

There is a high degree of risk associated with operating a sales organization whose knowledge of customers and associations is retained predominately in the heads of the sales individuals—particularly in situations where that person is the primary contact point for the customer. It is a risk that has seen many organizations suffer a significant downturn in their revenue when an individual departs, leaving a massive void in that person's place. The organization does not really know the customer beyond the past buying trends of those product reports and financial reports. It is left in a position where the customer can be targeted and signed by the competitors, since their past purchasing performance can be ascertained in a five-minute conversation by a competitor.

These are the hardest businesses of all to develop any form of systematic approach with as it is like trying to herd cats. They just aren't going to follow anything, as this has been their way of operating for many years. Typically I see the first touch point they experience of systems being the introduction of the CRM software—one that goes to the heart of who they are—and rarely do they embrace it with open arms. At that point the word "systems" become poison anytime the subject is raised.

Managing the risk of making no individual greater than the organization has not been a focus in the past. The marketplace was strong and the risk of departures mainly lay in keeping those people content in their roles. With the crisis, there have been extenuating circumstances where companies have had to let people go that were once valued employees. As those people left the business, so did the knowledge.

Companies today have learned how critical it is to manage the knowledge bases of their businesses and ensure they are retained by the companies and not the individuals. That shift alone would be one of the greatest challenges in cultural change to address, as it goes to the core of what companies have communicated in the past and how they need to operate in the future.

CRM is only a diminutive element of systems

When we make reference to systems we are talking about sales force systems, systems designed to meet the business requirements of the sales organization to manage the risk, productivity, behaviors, and knowledge of individuals, as well as effective tools for decision making. We are not talking about CRMs. They are just a diminutive element that contributes to the overall sales force system requirements.

In days gone by there were reports that were considered systems and they are in fact ineffectual. Any salesperson that has ever filled one in, knows it. I still see them to this day and those are the call reports. They are typically a page where sales individuals enter details of the calls they have made, along with the outcomes and comments. Some have tick boxes; others categorize products discussed. It is an amateur attempt at getting something from sales individuals to see what they are doing. Interestingly I have seen them in companies where CRM is installed, which means the software is not being used effectively or there is a major duplication of tasks.

That style of reports is referred to as one-way reporting. Once you get the report, there is literally nothing you can do with it, other than review it and file it. You will either file it in the round bin beside your desk or, if you are a compulsive hoarder, you will keep it in a filing cabinet.

The report does not link from one report to the other; it's just a summary (and very often of questionable content) of the week/month.

Most attempts at sales reporting revolve around salespeople giving their interpretation of the progress of a potential sale and even with definitions around those milestones; it's still the most ambiguous report you can gather from someone. Human nature will dictate the quality of the report based on whether the salesperson is under pressure for performance or excellence.

The following story will give all directors a clear understanding of the impact of management by individual versus management with systems.

When sales results can disguise impending disaster

A well-known financial institution with many years' successful trading experience entered into a new era with the appointment of new members of the board. The organization had been growing successfully through its seventy-plus years of trading and was one of the most respected institutions with a high level of brand recognition.

In recent years it was experiencing growth of 15 percent per annum, with excellent profits being returned to the shareholders. With the change of board members there came a change of senior executives within the organization and the incumbent CEO was asked to move on, as his vision for the organization was no longer that of the board. They wanted to take a new direction more beneficial to the shareholders.

At that time they also embarked on a restructuring process that saw a number of other influential executives depart the business voluntarily. The organization had a strong customer base and excellent growth momentum that would carry it into the future. With the board's new plans, it was poised to be the dominant player in the market for years to come.

New sales management was hired to take on a team of some forty-plus field salespeople and twenty internal salespeople. The sales management regime was considered to be people that were industry experts with long-standing reputations in the financial services market.

These were the people charged with the responsibility of bringing the board's vision to fruition. Members of the new sales management team had a very traditional approach: everything was done on the fly, with no strategic plans and little emphasis on documentation—anything to keep those sales figures coming in the door.

They created a lot of hype around themselves. The sales figures were certainly being achieved month after month. As the business continued to grow, it was soon time to make further changes. The board proposed a restructure of the sales force that would bring significant cost savings to the organization. This was embraced by the sales management, and they set about making those changes.

Unfortunately, the sales staff did not embrace the changes and became quite aggressive about the fact that their customers were being taken away from them as part of the restructuring. The sales figures started to falter as the disgruntled sales team became more focused on addressing their personal problems with the restructuring than with meeting the organization's goals.

As you would expect, the news spread among the organization's competitors, who immediately started making approaches to hire the disgruntled salespeople. Over a period of six to twelve months, fifteen salespeople left the organization and went to the competition. This in itself had a catastrophic impact on the business, since management had to hire and train new personnel and was not prepared for such changes to occur. They had assumed the salespeople would embrace the changes just as they had. They had developed no active plan to manage the change process other than holding conversations with the salespeople.

As the new hires entered the business, they were challenged to bring in the sales results of the past. Interestingly, once the departed salespeople had joined various competitors, they were also unable to repeat at their new employer the sales figures they had achieved in the past.

The upshot of the changes was that the organization lost $400 million of revenue within two years, which equated to 25 percent of its annual revenue. The downward spiral seemed unstoppable.

Exacerbating the problem were a large number of substandard loans, exposing the organization to major losses through debt recovery, and deals that had been written outside of organization policy, exposing the institution to potential litigation. The list went on.

On review of the business, the following factors were discovered:

- The sales figures were being initially generated by the momentum of the sales team, as well as the longevity and reputation of the business. The business was achieving its maximum capacity in the policies and processes set down for a financial institution. When the salespeople were placed under pressure to further increase sales, they started signing risky loans to keep the figures up. They used their selling skills internally to get the stamp of approval for loan-approval areas.

- The sales managers had elected to stop the salespeople recording all customer interaction on the long-standing CRM system, and there was a loss of eighteen months' information on customers. The new hires were unable to pick up with the customers, and the lack of knowledge of their background was seen by customers as poor service. Interestingly the departed salespeople (who had previously had access to this information) were now needing to rely on their memories of customers at their new employ and were also seen as giving bad service, as they did not remember the details like they had in the past.

- The management of the sales force was not focused on the use of systems. The managers believed people should operate autonomously. There was no follow up or checking to make sure personnel were operating as required by the organization.

- The new hires endured substandard inductions. The sales management had insufficient knowledge and resources to provide a professional induction. They also did not allocate sufficient time for the induction process. The salespeople were ill prepared to be in the market representing the organization, thereby diminishing the brand of the business.

- There was insufficient sales force reporting to alert management to any irregularities or potential problems in the behaviors of the salespeople.

- There were no standards of performance, guidance, or processes that supported both existing salespeople and new hires. They were operating on their own interpretations of what was required.

Needless to say, the sales management has since been restructured again. New professional management has been installed that is capable of managing behaviors, productivity, cultures, and knowledge management in a business. There have been risk-management initiatives installed to ensure that a professional team represents the brand in the market at all times.

Putting a value on systems

So the question is: what is the value of systems? To this organization, the new systems were worth $400 million (a substantial amount in anyone's terms). In your organization, you may assume an equivalent value of 25 percent of your revenue, at least. Most organizations will realize a 25 percent increase in revenue and good increases in earnings before interest and taxes (EBIT) when the right sales force systems are implemented and sustained.

The tasks sales managers need to focus on are working out the moneymaking line and then ensuring that salespeople work to the line. That requires sales managers to be at all times focused on salespeople's productivity and behaviors, ensuring that their time is best used to maximize sales results. They need to ensure that the company is best aligned to support the outcomes and not creating unnecessary barriers with the business.

Sales managers are required to not only to operate themselves, meeting both their day-to-day and strategic requirements, but also to lead their team members to operate in a similar manner within their designated areas of responsibility. Unlike any other management role in a business, you are working with a very rapidly shifting dynamic that is dictated by the customers.

The sales manager's role can be considered the most challenging and pressured environment of all, as they balance all the requirements each and every day. Some managers are dragged heavily into the day-to-day and do not have the time to step out and install the necessary systems that will result in easing the pressure that is their day-to-day life.

What takes priority defines the outcome

I was working with a business in the construction industry that had recently acquired several of its competitors. It had taken an immediate position of market dominance through the strategic acquisition of those other companies. The sales teams all used to be competitors and now were faced with sitting alongside each other as a team. The sales manager was front and center to what was a problematic merger, as he did not think through enough of the details in advance before the new team arrived.

The sales manager was a very organized person by nature and seen as the best person to lead the merger of teams. He was experienced, a good seller, and a person of admirable qualities.

The teams came together and within days, all hell broke loose as everyone was on a different page, doing different things, and the sales manager was the captain firefighter attempting to wrangle the team into way of doing things. His days were long, tiring, and full of pressure. He was dragged into the business and could see they were going to sink quickly. He was herding cats.

There were systems in place but not sufficient to keep people focused on the right tasks. We were invited in to do all the background work and install all the necessary systems and processes to ensure the effective operation of the sales organization. It was an intense six or eight weeks but with effort from everyone involved—it was achieved.

We then drew a line in the sand, stopped the team in the market, and re-inducted everyone on the systems. We nominated a couple of people to be ongoing reviewers to ensure that everyone had clarity.

The business made an immediate change and the sales manager was released to return to the tasks he did best of all—leading the sales team.

The systems had put in the base line that was required for effective management.

The outcome for the business: a successful merger of all teams and increasing revenue in just six months.

The systems implemented within an organization are the systems that underpin all those management requirements of a highly effective sales organization. These systems ensure that sales managers can operate effectively on a day-to-day basis while simultaneously meeting the strategic requirements of the organization. They confirm to salespeople exactly how they can grow the business, where to focus their efforts, and what level of consistency is required to deliver those results.

With these systems behind them, the salespeople are planning their success, not just stumbling along and hoping for it. There is operational effectiveness through the sales organization's activity, and overall the sales culture is one of proactive and planned behaviors that deliver growth.

It may well be that you have some systems in place, but insufficient systems to support a world-class sales organization. To refresh your memory about what world-class is and why you must strive to that standard, review these six points:

1. World-class means having a clear picture of success.

2. World-class means focusing on the things you can control.

3. World-class means avoiding excuses.

4. World-class means consistently performing at top levels.

5. World-class means believing in breakthroughs.

6. World-class means preparing for quantum leaps in performance improvement.

The implementation and use of the right systems will provide your sales organization with a quantum leap in performance improvement and profitable revenue increases, even if you already have some systems in place.

Chapter 11:

Sales Force Effectiveness - What Does It Really Mean?

This is arguably one of the most poorly used terms in business today as vendors attempt to align their products to the concept of sales force effectiveness. The three words combined have become buzzwords in recent years and many people have the concept on their minds—it is just their interpretations that vary.

If you do a quick search on Google, in the first page you will get a myriad of different definitions related to pharmaceutical industries, software, sales process metrics, and the list goes on. It really comes down to what people's first exposure to the terminology was, as to how they interpret everything they read thereafter.

The disillusionment of the terminology

In a recent survey of eight hundred senior executives by Sales Focus International, we uncovered some surprising facts about their interpretation of what sales force effectiveness actually meant to them.

- 53 percent stated it related to operation of a CRM system.

- 29 percent stated it related to the ability of a salesperson to close a deal (metrics).

- 10 percent had yet to decide.

- 8 percent stated it related to strategy through to execution with a focus on top-line revenue and bottom-line profit.

You can certainly see who has done the most marketing of the term. The actual answer is the commercial-orientated answer that reported just 8 percent in responses. That means that 92 percent of the market are missing the point of sales force effectiveness and more importantly, missing the point that can be putting significant revenues on their top and bottom lines.

Many vendors are attempting to align a single product to the concept of sales force effectiveness as it is something everyone wants—an effective sales force. The fact is, it is term that relates to the entire sales organization and not just one product. It has a series of contributing factors that, when all weighted and developed correctly, deliver sales force effectiveness (SFE).

People often fall short in their expectations when it comes to SFE as they are looking for simple solution. Hence they look for the simple solution of CRM software or sales training. Other people just don't understand sales forces enough to realize there are no simple solutions with such a complex problem.

CRM vendors have made themselves out to be the holy grail of SFE, but in fact the software is really only about 5 percent of what the requirements really are for genuine sales force effectiveness.

Certainly CRM has its place but, interestingly, its true capability is now overridden by the extensive bells and whistles added to the software in an attempt to have a point of difference in the market. Some systems have reached the point of analysis paralysis. There are that many different reports that can be generated from so many different angles. Salespeople have no hope of finding satisfaction in using it, as there is always a report stating they are not performing well.

The CRM software market is now an overcrowded market where everyone is attempting to make a unique and high-value product. Watching the pricing of CRM over the past few years, it has supported the commodity element, as pricing has dropped by greater than 50 percent on some products. Having worked with most brands of CRM, they are all very similar and if you can get people functioning with the software at the systems basic level, you could be in a slightly better place.

The focus of the CRM software is the pipeline report, which has become the focus of meetings and the catalyst for frustration through its unreliable forecasts for many organizations. The pipeline report is great for managing new business opportunities or larger order values, but once you attempt to align it with repetitive ordering associated with route selling, it fails dismally.

The pipeline report (whether software-based or using excel) is a quality report if it is set up correctly. In most cases it measures from first meeting through the various stages of qualification, presentation to close. What many fail to do is provide sufficient metrics within that process to be of value.

The other issue I see time after time is that the pipeline is not correctly aligned to the selling process/ranking and real information that is required. This makes the pipeline of considerably less value to the company and particularly the sales force members.

Senior executives are reliant on the figures from a pipeline for management reports, and often they are sleepless over the figures presented and the reality of what arrives in the order book. Other solid features are customer management, time management, and follow up to ensure that opportunities do not slip through—as long as they actually use the software properly!

The question is, do you need a CRM? Yes, but it's only a small part of the equation.

The other common default step for SFE is sales training. Those companies have latched on to the terminology, as their focus is on improving the performance within the sales process. Again, this is a very narrow view of what it is but a good hook for selling sales training.

You can teach people to be more effective in the sales process, but it will not produce results (as many people have experienced over the years) if everything else in the sales organization is not aligned correctly. Fundamentally, trainers are often asking the mice to run faster in the wheel. And people wonder why sales results are not forthcoming.

CRM software and sales training have their place within the sales force effectiveness requirement; however, each is only a small portion of the total equation.

The truth about sales force effectiveness

So what is sales force effectiveness? The following is a simple overview of what you would expect to see as part of the overall effort toward SFE.

- *Sales Strategy Execution* - Performance Management, Metrics, Sales Compensation, Quota Setting

- *Sales Strategy Support* - Sales Operations and Systems, Selling Messages and Tools, Recruiting and Career Paths, Capability and Development

- *Sales Strategy Development* - Marketing Strategy Alignment, Product/Service Offering, Segmentation and Targeting, Sales Strategy

- *Sales Force Organization* - Channel Coverage, Marketing, Sales, Service Roles, Organization Structure, Resource Deployment

Each of those segments gives a broad view of what should be included. Many people focus heavily on some areas but few go deeply enough in all areas. Typically people work on the points that have the most exposure in the business, and the balance is left to verbal leadership to guide people through the process or make decisions.

When we add the required commercial component and the sales manager is looked upon as a business unit manager, then the requirements are even broader through the sales organization. Our research can provide you with a good grounding in the overall requirements. This list is not in any specific order, just the subject matter that should be included.

- Sales strategy implementation plan at all levels through to individuals

- Human capital planning

- Cost control of sales head count and selling costs

- Knowledge management

- Risk management—human capital and financial

- CRM system implementation and pipeline management

- Sales compensation and rewards aligned to corporate goals

- Cross-organizational efficiency

- Performance management and quarterly reviews

- Brand management—human capital and collateral

- Analytical and strong follow-through on tasks

- Leadership based on set goals and requirements within team

- Role clarity

- Strong induction and educators

- Marketing systems and lead-tracking-measurement

- Defined selling practices

- Sales channel and distribution management

- Marketing intelligence and communication

- Budgeting/quota based on capacity planning, not historical

- Sales efficiencies on internal sales resourcing and reducing costs

- Metrics

- Integration between sales and marketing

- Market research—structured and reliable

- Pricing and Product Mix

As people scan down the list, often they tick off "yes" we have that in place. Everyone probably has some points in place to varying degrees of standards, but it comes back to the moneymaking line. It is not about whether you have those functions in place but whether they are correctly aligned to the moneymaking line to deliver the planned outcomes.

The other overriding factor is the interpretation of each element that defines the difference. How much depth is there in each of the contributing factors? Some people are happy to work at conceptual level and confirm to one and all they are doing everything that is required.

As they say, a little bit of knowledge is dangerous—and a lot is helpful.

The devil is in the detail and depth applied

I'll use a simple example of the term "territory management." To some it means identifying lines on a map and not going over your designated roads. To others it is a process of careful planning and review to ensure all opportunities are identified, targeted with a strategy, and converted along with existing customer management.

The secret to the success of SFE is applying the right emphasis on each point with the degree of depth required to produce the best outcome. It is important not to overcomplicate things but not simplify them to the point of being ineffective. The key is the alignment of each and every one to ensure there is no leakage in the process. It is not about operating a dinner buffet where you select what you want. It is about having each element carefully linked to each other and fully operational.

Underpinning all these points are a set of systems that support their effective and fluent operation in the business on a day-to-day basis. There is reporting that supports sound business decisions to ensure the strategic plan is translated in the market and the results are achieved in both top-line performance and bottom-line profit. Without all these points in place, you are not going to maximize the growth and profit of the organization.

This is what is required in all organizations, large or small. The responsibilities will be divided among individuals, depending on the structure and size of the sales organization. Some of the tasks are related to the pure sales manager's roles of coaching, guiding, and ensuring behaviors meet the minimum requirements. Others are related to more strategic elements that are then translated in detail to those that are interacting at customer level.

As a manager of a sales organization, this is what you must put in place, and then you can effectively manage to build a world-class sales organization.

You will also note in this insight into SFE that we have not mentioned sales cultures. Sales culture is not a process or a system. It is based on behaviors of individuals and their attitudes toward tasks that are required to be performed and those people they interact with. A poor sales culture does not allow SFE to exist. A good sales culture will adapt to SFE. People management is a product of SFE and the stumbling point for many sales organizations.

Chapter 12:
People, People, People

Management would be so much easier if we did not have to deal with people! This is a statement I hear over and over again when companies are frustrated with people and the cultures they need to deal with in their organizations.

Managing people is a difficult task and the more people you have to deal with, the more you understand that statement. A person's ability as a leader or manager of people is only revealed when you ask an individual to do something different or a specific task. If approached the right way, you get the outcome you desired. If you approach it the wrong way, you get resistance.

Hence the development of the laissez-faire leaders. Just as a reminder of what it means: the expression of laissez-faire leaders is defined as a non-authoritarian leadership style. Laissez-faire leaders try to give the least possible guidance to subordinates, and try to achieve control through less obvious means. They believe that people excel when they are left alone to respond to their responsibilities and obligations in their own ways.

Laissez-faire leaders create cultural problems

So fundamentally, they are stepping away from their responsibilities as a leaders and letting people do their own thing with small attempts to try to direct them but with often little success. When you attempt to ask these people to make changes and adopt new practices, you then are faced with the well-coined term "cultural problems." What this means is that people will not do what the company wants them to. They object to what is being asked of them or have a fundamental disagreement with the way the company is being run.

Cultural problems stem from a misalignment of people's beliefs with the company's beliefs. The role of a good leader is to assist people in understanding what is required of them and align their beliefs with the company's beliefs.

Thousands of hours of time have been dedicated to understanding how to do this appropriately and many hours have been lost in not achieving it. When you have cultural problems in a business, you have lower productivity and less outcomes being achieved.

Fundamentally it will always come down to people's attitudes. If they have good attitudes that want to engage in learning new things and doing things differently, you have a good culture (skill levels is not the priority, just attitude). If you have people that are resistant to new ideas and processes and want to draw things back to old practices, sustain existing practices, and generally not engage with what is on offer, you have a cultural problem and bad attitudes.

Depending on how deep the company's pockets are, they can decide what to do. With sales organizations the cost of a poor culture is a major financial hurdle, as you need to have people operating at their optimum at all times. A bad day for a salesperson becomes a financial loss to the business.

Over the years doing many turnarounds, decisions have had to be made over how to address the culture of a business. It was typically dependant on what was in place from the previous leaders and what outcomes were required in what time frame. In today's world, the same principles apply, as companies are very lean internally on resources and need to get the results from the marketplace.

If you are building a world-class sales organization, you cannot afford to carry dead weight with you. People need to understand the requirements for the future, have time to absorb what that means to them, and be guided on what they need to do as individuals; and then their attitudes will define what happens from there.

As many executives summarize it, "They have to work out if they are on the bus or not."

Identifying the telltale signs of cultural problems

Executives and sales managers who are looking to transform to world-class sales organizations often ask me, "What are the telltale signs of whether there will be cultural problems in adopting new systems and processes?"

The following list will give you some insight. You only need to have a couple of these points to put a red-flag warning in place.

- Little documented evidence of strategic plans exists at management level or sales plans at sales-individual level. People are used to working in a free-flowing environment and dealing with what comes up in the day with a general understanding to get revenue in the door.

- The general consensus is that salespeople are free spirits and you cannot document or systemize the how they do their roles. Selling is considered an art, not a science.

- The assumption is that salespeople are too busy to be completing paperwork or follow systems; they need to be on the spot with their customers, meeting the customer demands.

- No documented knowledge on the customer exists, apart from financial and product reports. CRM software was installed but the uptake of use is inconsistent, and low-quality information entered.

- Salespeople struggle to provide strategies and plans to grow their designated customers and/or territory apart from serving the customer.

- The teams are resistant to any form of reporting that would provide transparency to their performance.

- Salespeople hold within their designated territory large customer numbers that are impossible for one person to service and manage effectively.

- Salespeople are reluctant to have others interact with their customer bases and have a possessive nature toward their customers. They will refer to the customer as "my customer."

- Salespeople focus on a smaller number of customers from whom they can get quick responses to specials and offers to exceed quota and neglect other, more difficult customers.

- Strong resistance arises toward practices that are new to the business.

- New hires are often friends or people known to the business and already have exhibited traits that will see them adapt to the existing culture quickly.

- New hires from outside this group of associates often fail to deliver results and struggle to adapt to the culture in the business. Executives and sales managers often written off as bad hires rather than seeing issues in the business.

- The forecasting or pipelines of the salespeople are inaccurate and unreliable, but this does create good debate with the manager.

- Review meetings with major customers lack structure or purpose and are predominately verbal-based meetings.

- Metrics are based on financial reports and all others are unmeasurable key performance indicators that are open to personal interpretation.

If you have a few of those points in your sales organization then you will need to have a strong people person leading the team—a person that has the ability to influence the thinking of others, and bring them in line with the business's expectations in a commercially realistic timeframe.

The other question you also need to ask if you have attempted to install structure and systems in past (many have attempted at some stage): why won't the team adopt the use of systems?

- Do the systems of the business support the overall objectives?

- Does the cultural language of the business support the overall objectives?

- Do the systems add value to the salespeople and do they know how the systems contribute to their sales performance?

- Do the systems provide management with the information they need to make informed decisions and effectively manage the full responsibility of the sales organization?

Often I find that the systems that have been attempted were out of alignment—people failed to understand their value and they were seen as barriers to their performance, not assistance. Commonly salespeople have been told to use them, not coached and guided on how to use them and why.

Identifying the culture of a sales organization

You also need to give consideration to the over cultural of the organization. This can have a major effect on what the sales organization is attempting to achieve. Within organizations there are some different types of cultures which affect how you will implement the sales culture. It is important to understand the existing cultures, as they will impact how you make any necessary changes to the sales organization. These are some of the most common ones you will experience:

Academy Cultures

Employees are highly skilled and tend to stay in the organization while working their way up the ranks. The organization provides them with a stable environment in which employees can develop and exercise their skills. These cultures commonly occur in large organizations that have the resources to invest heavily in their employees and develop them over the long term. These are very secure environments for employees and they encourage learning attitudes. Employees are easy to educate and readily adopt new practices when they are encased in learning and career development.

These are great cultures for creating world-class sales organizations.

Highflier Cultures

Employees are free agents who have highly prized skills. They are in high demand and can rather easily get jobs elsewhere. They are people that seek freedom and are not drawn to structure. They are the epitome of the common man's view of a salesperson.

This type of culture exists in fast-paced, high-risk organizations, such as investment banking, advertising, and commission-only sales environments. These cultures are the hardest cultures to manage, as the people are extremely temperamental and will depart the moment they do not get their own way. Some have likened managing them to the managing a group of two-year-old children.

This is a problematic culture and great leadership is required to bring about any form of change.

Club Cultures

The most important requirement for employees in this culture is to fit into the group. Usually employees start at the bottom and stay with the organization for an extended period of time. A decision to leave is similar to getting a divorce. They are loyal to their superiors and will follow their directions without question. The organization promotes from within and highly values seniority. These are often cultures in law firms and family businesses where the head of the family or firm is seen as the leader. These cultures only respond to change when the leader fully endorses the change in both words and actions.

The leader will define the outcome by the congruency between his/her verbal communication and actions. Typically this exists in entrepreneurial businesses and privately owned companies.

Fortress Cultures

Employees in these cultures don't know if they'll be laid off or not. They worry about the effect a change of management will have on their roles. These organizations often undergo massive reorganization or are led by people that have a desire to start projects of change but fail to see them through. There may also be a high level of turnover at senior executive level. The staff are very apprehensive toward anything new and develop a culture of sitting out trends. There are many opportunities to bring about change for those with timely, specialized skills, and change focuses on making the most of those opportunities. The key is to move quickly through the initial change process.

This is the most common culture a new sales manager will take over, as it is one of the most common cultures in the market today, particularly following the global financial crisis. The uncertainty leads to the fortress culture.

This is a difficult culture to work with and will require relentless efforts from the executive and sales manager to bring about the transformation. No one individual can succeed in this environment—it takes a dedicated team of people.

Traditional Cultures

Employees in these cultures are set in their ways and have been doing the same tasks for many years. They have been successful over long periods of time and have had little exposure to other methods of operation. They constantly reference experiences from the past and quickly justify why the past was more successful. measures of success are based on consistency and longevity of customer relationships rather than growth. They constantly explain to new management that "this is the way we do things here" and often threaten departure if the status quo is altered. These cultures are very common where management changes have been extremely low over the years.

Again, this is a difficult culture to change and will need careful guidance and a strong executive team to bring about the changes. Typically once they have a few wins and people see the value in the changes, they will engage and develop a good energy behind the transformation when it is managed correctly.

In a sales organization you will be confronted by the culture that you need to manage on a day-to-day basis. That existing culture will determine the degree of effort that will be required on your part to develop it into the culture you need in order to deliver results. Cultures must be managed in every conversation and communication, not just at an annual event or in the statement each month from the CEO.

You can have all the systems and processes in the world but if you don't have the right culture, you will not get the results. It's like trying to win a race with a three-legged race horse.

How cultures are created

The following tale was told in one of my earlier books, Get Sales Focused. All traditional managers should be aware of it, since they may well be sitting in the cage or be about to be recruited to join the cage. This is a timeless tale of the evolution of an organization culture. I have yet to see a better description of one.

A Cage Full of Monkeys

Have you ever wondered how an organization creates a culture and how it arrives at its current state? Here is a tale that will better assist you to understand the development of the organization culture.

Start with a cage containing five monkeys. In the cage, hang a banana on a string and put a footstool under it. Before long, a monkey will go to the stairs and start to climb toward the banana. As soon as he touches the stairs, spray all of the monkeys with cold water.

After a while, another monkey will make an attempt with the same result—that all the apes are sprayed with cold water.

Continue this through several more attempts. Pretty soon, when another monkey tries to climb the stairs, the other monkeys will try to prevent it.

Now, abandon the cold water. Remove one monkey from the cage and replace it with a new one. The new monkey will see the banana and want to climb the stairs.

To his horror, all of the other apes will attack him. After another attempt and attack, he will realize that if he tries to climb the stairs, he will be assaulted.

Next, remove another of the original apes and replace it with a new one. The newcomer will go to the stairs and be attacked. This time, the previous newcomer will take part in the punishment with enthusiasm.

Again, replace a third of the original apes with a new one. The new one will make it to the stairs and be attacked as well. Two of the four apes that beat him will have no idea why they are not permitted to climb the stairs or why they are beating the newest monkey for doing it.

After replacing the fourth and fifth original apes, all of the apes that have been sprayed with cold water have been replaced.

Nevertheless, no monkey ever again approaches the stairs. Why not? Because that's the way it's always been around here. And that's how organization culture begins...

This little story applies to the culture of management and the culture of the sales organization.

Keeping focused on the outcomes

When transforming a sales organization, the outcome must be for improvement that will deliver top-line or bottom-line performance. The transformation in the processes, structure, or methods must focus on profit being the output. Profit is what owners and shareholders expect. At the end of the day, that is the overriding focus that is in place.

Through the transformation process, you must respect the people you are asking to change. You need to make it clear that you will support everyone and assist them in developing and growing within the culture. For those that are passive-aggressive or outright detractors, you can make it clear that the journey will be more difficult for them. You must be clear in your mind of what you want to achieve and how it will operate, then ensure that it is documented and workable every day.

This is not a vision statement. I am referring to having a working project plan with deliverables and milestones so you know when you are on or off track as a sales manager and executive team. You cannot just start into the process and pop your head up occasionally to see where you are going. The more structure in the project, the more likely the outcomes will be achieved.

I would say that identifying what has to be done initially is 80 percent of the project. But once that identification phase is complete, it is just 10 percent of the project plan. The sequence of the transformation within the project plan is vital to the overall success of the outcome. It is not about picking the easy subjects first and then working through to the hard ones.

It is about addressing each of the points as they impact upon each other in such a way that the sales organization can be transformed and does not aggravate problems in the business unnecessarily.

The other key is to keep everyone focused on facts and not allow personalities or personal interpretations to overwhelm the transformation. Your success in managing the sales culture will be your success in building a world-class and effective sales force.

Chapter 13:

I Purchased CRM Software But They Just Don't Use It

This is a question statement that I hear time after time from companies. Some have tried several different brands of software and still are not getting the outcomes the desire.

As indicated earlier, many organizations relate to CRM software as sales force effectiveness. They have set about implementing the software for the purpose of gaining better customer management, sales force management and opportunity management, believing that is what effectiveness means.

CRM fails big time for many companies

Many organizations report that the implementation of the CRM was not successful or are less than enthused in the results from it. Moreover, they have been confronted with the problem of a low level of adopters of its use and cultural problems abound each time the word CRM is used.

Many blame the software itself but, in all fairness to the software companies, in most cases it has nothing to do with the software. Most of the software on the market does the task required, some better than others. Having used and implemented many different brands of CRM software, I have yet to see any of them causing the problems they are often said to have caused. Often they simply amplify the underlying problems in the sales organization that have been left unaddressed over time.

The actual issue with the software is related to people, not technology. It's an organizational issue that needs to be managed. You can have the simplest and easiest-to-use software in the world; that will still not guarantee that people will use it.

Although the case for having a CRM is about as logical as one can get, it is an implementation of software like no other in an organization. If you implement software in the finance division, the software is seen as part of a process—an inanimate process where debtors are processed and creditors are processed. There is no personality to the entries; its just cash in/cash out.

The naked sales force

CRM, however, asks for your team to stand naked and show all their knowledge and wares to the world within the sales organization for each of their accounts. If you look at the background of many of those organizations, they have applauded the salespeople for their relationships, their knowledge of the customers, and their value to the organization. This is their security blanket for employment. As long as they have that lynch pin in place, they have jobs. Organizations have cultivated that culture for many years. They have praised, rewarded. and honored those individuals that were able to mystically bring in the business, the customers, and the relationships that kept the engine of the organization operating.

There have been organizations that have prized the person that could pull the rabbit out of a hat and save the year-end figures by securing the big deal. These people could get business where no man or woman dared to tread. They had the magic ability to just get those deals. No one questioned how they did it; they just applauded the outcome.

At the national conferences, they are the legends who can say or do anything and still keep shining. They are the bigger-than-life personalities that seem to know everyone. They put in a call and you have access to accounts you never thought you could penetrate.

In former days, these people were masters of sales and the art of selling. It was magical and exciting. Their sales managers could trust them to deliver. They took years to develop these skills and contacts and guarded them like the crown jewels. Their references to customers contained high levels of protectionism. They spoke of "my customers" and "my accounts." They assumed they must be the sole points of communication with the customers so the relationships could be managed. They were the heros when things got complicated with the customers through accounts or operations; they were the glue that kept it all together.

Organizations have hired sales individuals and managers based on their relationships and intimate knowledge of customers. During the hiring process, the compensation package was developed around the customer knowledge they could bring to the table.

Some of you will see this as a distant memory in how teams were run and others will be thinking, "Gee, that is us right now!" There are more in the "right now" category than you might imagine.

We wanted black and now we want red

Now management comes along and says, "We want all your contacts, customer knowledge, and communication with customers logged in the CRM. We are going to have all that knowledge centralized so we can see exactly what is going on and share the information with others in the team and across the organization." The salespeople go into convulsions as they are asked to strip and bare their all, so that the whole organization can see exactly what and how they do what they have done under cloak for many years.

The message from management has changed so significantly that the salespeople immediately feel distrust (as in the fortress culture). Some may even relate to this request as if they are being prepared to be sacked. Any idiosyncrasies they have, any ounces of distrust or personality challenges with management, come rising to the top as they are immediately on the defensive.

In the world of cultural change, that is about as great an impact as you will see. Their complete experience of communication and process has been up-ended. You can counsel them all you'd like, but the clash of communication from the past is too great; they will not recover. Some will elect to leave the company; others will attempt to just sit this one out. Where a club culture is in place, they may attempt to do some entries on the CRM; however, they will opt for the least amount of information possible until corrected.

I once talked with a company executive who said he operated a CRM. When I asked about the system and its functionality, I found it was quite a unique approach. He had the salespeople fill in call sheets (old style) and fax them through to a secretary, who then set about entering all the information to the system under each contact's name.

The salespeople had no access to the system, just a list of names and addresses of their accounts they were responsible for. The system had no readable format from other computers outside of the main one operated by the secretary. The secretary did not prepare any reports from the system or send copies to the salespeople. The system had never been tailored to their business requirements and was in an off-the-shelf format. But they would hold their hand on their hearts and swear they were operating a CRM!

Imagine the duplication of costs associated with the way they ran that system and its value back to the organization, which was nil.

In other organizations there will be similar stories where sales individuals have never been good at paperwork and reports. Over time, paperwork has been just been allowed to slip. Often the operations administration will pick up on the problems and fix them as they come through. A person with poor work habits that is asked to become organized with time management and follow-up calls registered against accounts will not do it. That is just not going to happen without excessive management time.

People who are low adopters of technology will also be challenged—not because the software has an issue, but because they don't turn on the computers to start with.

Some CRM implementers attempt to say that the process works better where you have a structured sales process. Yes, that will assist a little, but it will not resolve the problems of the culture ingrained in sales individuals. The culture is far stronger than any sales process.

So with just a few examples, you can start to see the trend of challenges that confront CRM implementation over any other software you are likely to install in an organization. It all comes down to the pattern of behavior and culture that is in place before the CRM is installed.

Technology does not manage cultural change

The CRM consultants are technology people who will detail the implementation based on standard sales processes for industry profiles and some tailoring. They are not trained in cultural change and are not cultural change specialists, nor should they be.

Remember, if the software is not working for you, then your culture is the most likely cause. If you are considering implementing CRM, you need to know where your culture fits in relation to the needs of working with the CRM, then how big that gap is and what steps need to be taken to bring them closer together.

Here is an interesting story and something you can all try when you are considering CRM.

I was once speaking with a national company regarding the underperformance of its team that had been an ongoing trend for the previous two fiscal years. The company had a number of major issues that would need some deep surgery to repair. Speaking with a prospective client one day, he advised us that he was not concerned over the culture of the business and the other items related to sales force management. His priority was to install the CRM, as he believed that would resolve most of issues with the team and its management.

We suggested that before he expended the funds for the CRM, he might ask his team to send him an email each evening outlining what they had achieved for the day, so he could start to get an insight into their activities, as that would assist him in tailoring the CRM. The key was to make sure they sent the email every day so he could have a thorough understanding. He agreed that this was a good idea and sent out the requirement to everyone.

He telephoned us about ten days later and advised us that he was having real issues getting his team to send the emails. If he got one, it had very little information on it. The CRM had advised him not to do it but he was concerned that, if they would not send an email, they would not fill in the CRM. As he said those words, he realized that this was why we had asked him to do it.

To the frustration of the CRM vendor, his sale was put on hold for a few months while the culture was sorted out to be better prepared to accept the change. There was considerable work done in advance to make sure the implementation was successful and the adoption of users was high.

In contrast:

I watched the implementation of a major brand of CRM to a large insurance organization which was grounded in relationships and secrecy of sales activities. It was an institution that was rife with subcultures. Through the process of providing training to the organization, it was clear that the business and managements approach was to gently coddle people into the acceptance of new methods. Those who were resistant received special attention with increased coddling in an attempt to nurture them and allow them time to grasp what was being asked of them. The salespeople were praised because they were considered to be the key to all relationships within the business and the only reason customers came to the business at all. On surveying the customers, however, the exact opposite was found to be true.

When it was announced that the CRM was to be implemented, management appointed a committee to manage the process. The first assignment was to document the sales process as the core function of the CRM and the opportunity management. The CRM vendor was unable to document a process based on their organizational practices, and the committee were unable to agree on a standard process. The CRM provider could not recommend a standard process. This task seemed to require an endless number of changes to the point that the CRM vendor declared something had to be agreed on and it could not be debated any longer. Getting the team to design and agree on the sales process was like asking the alcoholic to look after a liquor store. It was not about what they were doing; it should have been about what they were supposed to be doing as an effective sales organization.

When the software was finally customized, a group of people were nominated as the trial workers to ensure it was correct before the rollout commenced for all employees. The debate over the sales process and how they did business continued. As changes were made, more were identified. The business improvement process was not complete, so all the problems associated with administration compounded the issues of the sales process, causing greater problems in the CRM.

It was decided after some time to roll it out across the organization. Probably, the patience of the CRM vendor was wearing thin (and we would not have blamed them).

The rollout, as expected, was less than acceptable. Many users did not adopt the system. The usage levels were intermittent at best. The few good users had quickly dwindling interest, as they were a minority.

Management was responding with more counseling sessions in an attempt to coddle people into action. They had invested many thousands of dollars and were under the scrutiny of their senior executive regarding the success of the project.

The CRM vendor was under pressure because the project was not gaining momentum or engagement. The decision was made that people just had to use the CRM no matter what. The instruction from the CRM vendor to its client was to advise all the staff that "if it's not in the CRM, then it's not true and will not be discussed." This mantra was sent across the organization, and salespeople were threatened with a big stick if they dared mention a customer or sales opportunity that was not shown in the CRM or if a sale arrived that was not in the system.

This is a common reason that people jump to the conclusion that CRM does not work. It is easier to blame the software than the actual people charged with the responsibility of its implementation. With the growth of the market in CRM, there are many underskilled people involved in the implementation— very few that are experts in sales process to the level required. That is not the vendor doing the implementation, but the people internal to the organization.

CRM vendors do not do change management and nor do they often write a sales process that bring about improvement requirements in a sales organization. They can provide standardized processes that should fit an organization, but each location will have different requirements based on its business practices, strategy, and emphasis areas within the process, according to the maturity of its customer base.

The organization must have the culture developed to such a point that CRM is another step in a series of accepted changes, not the catalyst for change. There are important behaviors and processes that must be in place before the CRM is even contemplated by the team.

Chapter 14:

Sales and Marketing - A Match Made in Heaven?

For true sales force effectiveness and a world-class sales organization, marketing must be included in the process. The more marketing is utilized for the generation of leads, the more important it is for sales force effectiveness.

If you are serious about growing any business, then you must have the marketing component working in harmony with your sales organization.

The chicken or the egg syndrome

There is always discussion over whether the key to any organization's growth is sales or marketing. Is it the salespeople that are signing deals or the marketing team that are creating the awareness? There is a place for both, but that place is defined by customers, the industry, and the involvement of each in the process. Where the consumer or domestic market is your target audience, then certainly the need for marketing is the lead process for growth. Your target is a mass audience with multiple-point purchasing, so marketing is the only real way to reach those people.

Where your target audience is corporate or small to midsize businesses, then there is a lower requirement on marketing and a higher degree of emphasis on sales individuals. At no point does either become redundant in the process; the relative emphasis is defined purely by target audience behavior and finding the right balance. From an organizational perspective, you have to be very clear about your target audience and the volume of targets you wish to reach. Quite often we see emerging businesses direct enormous sums of money toward their target audiences with little return being achieved. This can be the case regardless of whether the target is a domestic or a business audience.

Born from the same cast

Like sales, marketing is often seen as a mystical art form, with results changing on a day-to-day basis, dependant on extraneous factors ranging from other advertisements to whether the moon and stars were lined up that day.

In years gone by, when reviewing sales and marketing processes within organizations, I often quietly wonder who can spin more lines, the sales force or the marketing department. When poorly managed, both have a plethora of lines and stories that can be convincing to the uninitiated, frustrating to the experienced, and amusing to the well initiated.

Both the sales and the marketing departments have grown from very similar beginnings and certainly have caused senior executives equal amounts of anxiety over the years. Both were created in gray environments, meaning they were not accountable for the results and it was all about big personalities and individuals with no real business content in conversation other than attracting customers.

Marketing has been renowned for the advertising pitch: an ability to create passion for the product with a significant price ticket attached for providing their service. Rarely would you see a presentation that talked about expected return on investment. Sales were renowned for the pipeline report: an ability to create a false sense of security regarding the level of potential business that will be signed. Both end in disappointment, frustration, and certainly a diminishing level of respect as the goalposts are shifted throughout each conversation.

For both sales and marketing, times have changed and the art/science debate is a thing of the past. Organizations will not and should not be expected to tolerate an inadequacy of performance in either business unit.

Getting the relationship right

The careful alignment of their activities so they dovetail perfectly to each other is critical from both the customer's perspective and the financial costs of operating both areas of the business. Any review process needs to consider how much activity the marketing department undertakes within the sales process and how much the sales department is fulfilling.

Usually you will find that there is a gap between the two which is an area of great cost and profit leakage.

Sales Focus International has researched this extensively and identified seven crucial steps in the buying process. This is not to be confused with the sales process. We are talking about the actual buying process from a customer perspective where a customer becomes aware of a product through to actually purchasing it. Where a buyer is taken through each of those steps in sequence, using an approach that is focused on their behaviors, the results are exceptional: organizations realize an excellent return on their investments.

Unfortunately for many organizations, the buyer process is disrupted in several areas or is out of sync with the buyer; therefore, the results can be variable. Some organizations do not invest enough in marketing; others invest too much. Some over-support the sales process, while others starve the sales force of leads, inhibiting their ability to secure sales.

The other factor often contributing to some of the anxiety generated by these two departments is the incongruent message between sales and marketing, which frustrates the buyer and stops the purchase. Both marketing and sales can be and should be operated through an efficient structure that is a predictable and reliable method, removing the gray area or mystic quality from the process.

It can never be a finite practice as there are always some variables; however, its predictability can be calibrated within inches instead of miles. Considerable savings can be made where the structure spans both sales and marketing.

As a senior executive or sales manager (depending on the reporting lines in your organization), you must have in place the control factors that will effectively manage these two important areas in concert with each other. You must have the right balance of what is required to attract the buyers and what is required to allow them to purchase.

There are two famous catchcries that come from these two areas, which alert you immediately to the problems:

- Marketing: "We have generated an enormous number of leads, but sales never sign them up."

- Sales: "We never get any leads from marketing, so what is the point?"

The first message is that sales and marketing are out of sync with each other, with profits being wasted on several levels. It might be that the salespeople see no value in the leads being generated and are just wasting them. It might also be that the salespeople do not know how to convert the leads, or even that marketing's reference to leads versus sales' reference is different—that difference being the qualification. What you can be confident of is that you have lost money on the marketing department and advertising, and on the sales department—and their cost of sale has increased. There is no joy until this aspect is adjusted so as to maximize both areas' performance.

The second message is the question as to whether the salespeople are reactive or proactive. What value is the marketing department to the buyer's process? Is its role to actually generate leads or just awareness? Again, the requirement for an adjustment that maximizes both areas performance is a priority.

So who actually creates the opportunity for the business? Some consultants say it's the marketing department; others say it's the sales department. Neither is right and neither is wrong. The answer depends purely on your industry and product and there is no one-size-fits-all approach. The only commonality is the seven-step buyer process, starting with awareness of your products through to purchasing. For some companies heavy emphasis is applied by marketing to create the awareness and drive the sale to a certain point where sales can take over. Others require a lower level of interaction from marketing to draw the buyer into the purchasing process.

A standard marketing process that is applied in many organizations is the development of product brochures. Information sheets show potential buyers the features and benefits of the products.

It's an institution in marketing for many organizations. The question that arises from these brochures is: if you want the salespeople to sell consultative or solution style, why do you arm them with the redundant selling tool of features and benefits? We all know that salespeople will say what is written on the brochures, so you need to be careful what they are using as reference materials. Whether the brochure is now in an electronic format or however it is made available to customers, the message and selling practice must be congruent.

Are you blindly following the practices of the past and not updating your approach to both sales and marketing to be in tune with the new buyer processes and new marketplace?

Is marketing aligned to the new marketplace?

The marketplace has changed, customers have changed their demands, and certainly the selling style has to change to be aligned with those customers. Customers are demanding more value than ever from their purchases and solid business cases to make decisions. They must be able to determine easily the business propositions or validate the reasons to buy.

Business-to-business selling is far more involved and detailed in the current market and will continue to be that way into the future. Buyers are learning new ways of looking at vendor offerings and are closely scrutinizing each of those offers. Lowest prices may win some deals for short gains but overall, vendors are astute and need to purchase quality and durable products in all situations.

Organizations need to consider what changes marketing have made to stay in tune with the buyer. Are you inhibiting your sales force by sending them out with a mixed message? Sell consultatively and tailor your products specifically to customers' needs. So why ask the sales team to take out a brochure that communicates features and benefits? What message is in the marketing material? What message is in the sales documentation? How in touch with the customer are both business units?

Often an internal review is best to define the consistency of the messages that are being applied for sales and marketing and to regularly review that they are in sync with the market.

Marketing effectiveness

The other important factor that relates directly back to sales force effectiveness is measurement. Successful measurement of marketing and sales means having in place the right process and reporting that informs you on how to improve their performance rather than giving you answers about outcome only.

Such reports should give you information on how to make the necessary adjustments within each process to improve the outcome. Like the measurement applied to the sales process for metrics/conversion ratios, the marketing department should have transparency of its processes and its performance. Certainly the outcome is important, but you need to make informed decisions to improve the performance within the process, otherwise you are not in a position to deliver an improved outcome.

Organizations must have in place the measurements to assist them to maximize returns on both business units and demonstrate the congruency from one to the other to avoid leakage in opportunity and cost, and only then can they increase the profitability of the organization.

Chapter 15:

How are you playing the game?

As reviewed earlier in the book, there are different generations of management that are applied to sales organizations, all with the philosophy of gaining performance. Each have their own unique set of priorities applied according to the sophistication of the sales organization.

Appropriately, several years ago Harvard Business Review[1], a leading business journal, investigated sales organizations closely as to their behaviors and degrees of competitiveness in the market. Much like the Sales Focus International research, they were able to identify groups with specific behaviors that defined how competitive they were in the market. Researchers were able to ascertain four specific levels of performance within sales forces. Each of these levels was directly related to the sales force systems in place and the management style that was applied to the sales organization.

The underlying component of success in the sales organization is the management. The managers must have the ability to put in place the right processes and methodologies and be able to coach the team to become a high-performance sales organization. The consistency of the manager's performance will be reflected in the consistency of the sales team. The maturity of the sales organization will define how well the company will play the game in the market. The maturity is gained not through years of experience, but rather through sophistication in how the organization goes about doing business on a day-to-day basis.

We have aligned the research from Harvard Business Review (HBR) with a sporting scenario, as most people relate well to this and see the correlation between business and playing the game.

Which team are you playing for?

Most people have been exposed to the different levels of sport through football games, either by playing or watching. It does not matter what type of football it is; the levels are the same within each of the different disciplines.

Many of us start sports in junior high school. It's our first introduction to team sports. Someone guides us on how we must perform at different levels.

Level 1. In junior high school, children play football with only a few basic rules and boundaries applied. Basically, there are the field goals, the boundary line around the outside, and some basics of where people should be standing and the general direction they should be taking the ball. The children are encouraged to play fairly. It's all about developing relationships with the others and maintaining the spirit of the game. Any mistakes are okay, unless they endanger another child. Children are encouraged to display their talents and give it their best shot. The coaches are volunteers giving the limited time they have each week to grouping the children at the start of the game and managing them through their temper tantrums. They attempt to focus the children back to the task of playing the game.

HBR writes that Level One companies are those that are anti-process, though what they really lack is a single standard process. Everyone does their own thing, in their own way. The company may not be unsuccessful but it is certainly creating enormous opportunity for competitors to take market share from them.

If you look back at the research by Sales Focus International (SFI) earlier in the book, this is referred to as the first generation of sales managers.

Level 2. A child may then progress to high school football. The number of rules increase around what is right or wrong when you play the game, and there is some technique applied in how the game is played. The children are trained in the basics of kicking the ball, aiming for goals, handling the ball, and some basic tactics to overcome competitors.

The coach (or manager) is a person often paid a nominal sum with many other responsibilities outside just football. The team seemingly works well and does have some wins, but they have also many other opportunities that are not pursued. The game still is about enjoyment with slightly tighter boundaries and rules.

In corporations, these are categorized by SFI as second-generation sales managers.

During this process there is a smaller group of people within that group that then become more dedicated to the game and the games are a stepping-stone to professional sports. They may gain scholarships to college and one day join a professional team. These people craft their skills and learn more tactics and methods to be successful. They study their sport and want to excel in it. They are a minority group looking to rise to the top.

HBR writes that a Level Two company is one that expects its sales force to follow a process, but the process is not monitored or measured. This describes nearly 50 percent of businesses operating in the world today, whether SME or large corporations.

These are defined by SFI as third-generation sales managers in its research.

Level 3. A person then becomes a player in a professional minor league, where there are professional coaches and players who are serious about winning. These coaches have experience as players. The players look for a team that will assist them in excelling. In these games, sets of boundaries are established. Players closely review the rule book to ensure that they comply with the rules. The coaches establish the boundaries and conduct for each person in specific positions on the field. They review what has gone wrong after games and who did not follow the rules.

HBR writes that Level Three companies are those that typically enforce use of a standard process, but typically look backward and therefore are constantly exposed to missing opportunities in changing markets.

These are defined by SFI as fourth-generation companies in its research.

Level 4. A person then becomes a professional player in a major league. The professional coach is a highly experienced player in his/her own right. The coach sets boundaries and role functions and focuses on every specific detail of each position, ensuring that the person is best trained and fit to complete the role. The team is trained every day; strategies are made for every game; past plays are reviewed closely. All the team members know exactly what they have to contribute and are measured for their contribution.

These teams are formidable competitors to beat in the market. They excel in all areas of the skills and disciplines required, making them impenetrable forces. When they focus on winning new customers and staving off attacks of their existing customers, they win!

HBR writes that Level Four companies are those companies that dynamically monitor and provide feedback on sales force use of systems and standard process. These companies modify systems with ongoing changes as they detect even minor changes in the market. These companies are formidable competitors.

These are defined by SFI as fifth- and sixth-generation companies in its research.

In consideration of this information, you need to objectively consider where you are playing the game. Are you playing the game for enjoyment or to be a highly competitive organization? As you can read from the different levels, high-performance teams don't just happen. They are highly trained and effectively managed individuals who are best placed to succeed.

Winners and losers

The cost associated with having a high-performance team versus a low-performance team is the same when you take into account salary packages and direct costs associated with employees. The difference is that the high-performance team delivers considerably higher top-line revenue than the low-performance team. The high-performance team ensures the longevity of the business through changing markets, whereas the low-performance team is a high risk to the business, which many have experienced through the crisis.

[1]   Barry Trailer and Jim Dickie, "Understanding What Your Sales Manager Is Up Against," Harvard Business Review (June 2006).

Chapter 16:

The Business Case for Transformation

Through reading the book to this point, you may be giving serious thought to whether your organization wants to be a world-class sales organization. You may be considering as an individual as to whether you want to lead a world-class sales organization. There may be thoughts over what the process would deliver in real tangible outcomes if it were embarked on.

There have been many projects or theories started in companies over the years that have fallen flat for a myriad of reasons—some through lack of internal support, others through change of management, and for some, bigger issues just hit the board table and had to be prioritized.

What we see for sales organizations is that there is typically lack of understanding of effort required to complete the project and clarity over the financial outcomes. People commence a project, not realizing the time, effort and resources required to deliver the outcomes. They start into the project, they may hit barriers through cultural issues, and the project goes off scope quickly. They are caught in the project—not delivering the project.

Before starting any project, the other consideration is the financial impact. Cost is one side of the equation but the other is gain. What top-line and bottom-line results will be seen if the project is embarked on? This question in particular needs to be answered before any project commences in a sales organization.

Projects that fall over

When projects are started using internal reviews and resources, they often fail on all those points. People get excited (particularly after going to a seminar) and start attempting to make changes. They have not considered the full impact of what is going to happen or may not have the experience and reference structure to know what will happen. What can be seen as a shining light to one person may be seen as a train coming to another. A project implemented too quickly can become a false start. I am sure you can all relate to that in your working careers where you have been affected by the false-start project.

The internal review is also problematic, as you are seeing the business from your own perspective and not reviewing it against best-practice. Industry practice means that you do what your competitors also do. And businesses' best-practice is what the wider group of businesses does as best-practice that will give you the edge. There is a great case study at the end of this book in relation to this.

The internal review will fundamentally reinforce the obvious things that you already know but not put you far enough forward that it will make a rudimentary difference to how you operate. There will be improvements but not the quantum leap that is required.

Stepping back and getting the real facts

The independent review is going to achieve a more thorough and analytical view of the business and the experience of other industries in order to investigate and consider alternatives that will enhance profitability. It also will remove the issues of personalities that exist within the business and will provide the opportunity to explore all areas in a relatively unhindered manner. The expression "relatively unhindered" is used, as it will depend entirely on the culture of the business and the introduction used by the executive to announce the person's presence and objective. Where this is done correctly, employees will assist without hesitation and provide the necessary information and untainted insights needed for analysis.

The review process is the step that defines the business case.

The review process is a project within itself, so it is looking clinically at the contributing areas that will be required for the transformation to be effective. It will go through all areas that affect sales force effectiveness and provide a measure of what is currently contributing positively and what needs to be improved. It will demonstrate clearly what the financial outcomes that should be attained from the transformation project and some insight into cost reductions through improved systems and process. It will establish all the reporting requirements and metrics. It will create a list of priorities for attention.

During the review process, a number of different approaches are applied to gain the required information.

Questionnaires - a questionnaire is provided to nominated people related to sales and marketing to gain insight into the tasks and processes they are completing, and into the details of reporting. This process will also start the initial look at potential cultural change barriers that may be experienced through the implementation project.

Interviews: Cultural and Process - from the questionnaires, a number of people will be selected for interviewing to gain further insight into their functionality and company processes. Most importantly, this will provide insight into the cultural impact on the company and potential barriers to change.

Measurement - a review of the measurements, including ones typically not considered to extract additional information that can be reviewed and used to for analysis in relation to growth. There are specific metrics that can be applied to understand the full capacity of the business in relation to the sales organization. This will also define new business acquisition requirements and existing business resource requirements.

Examination List - a list of all the contributing factors that will need to be examined that will contribute to the sales organization being transformed and prioritize what needs to be done. Depending on the organization there are some fifty to seventy points for examination.

Flow review - a review of the flow of primary internal processes, both documented and verbal, is conducted to ascertain all potential profit leakage areas. This is documented for review and clarity and to form the basis of any further work post the business case. This flow review is a combination of walking exercises where you follow each step through the business and also through interviews.

Quality of Application - as noted earlier in the book, the application of sales management practices is a contentious point with often one's personal interpretation of how it should be performed being quite different than best practice. The application of some fifty-plus points within sales management needs to be reviewed to ensure it is to the required depth and intensity so that it has a positive contribution.

Benchmarking - there will be a series of elements within the business that can be benchmarked for performance.

There are several other processes that are applied and they will depend entirely on the type of business you operate and the products/services provided to your customer.

The analysis of degree of effort required to transform the organization and potential profit is completed based on the findings above. All this information is collated and reviewed to establish the business case.

No business case-no transformation

Executives need to be confident of the business case for the transformation to commence. There has to be a commercial reason why this project should be embarked on.

Timeline to complete the business case

This review process should take approximately two to three weeks to complete, depending on the complexity of the business and the geographical areas covered. The timeline differs from site to site, through the scope of the engagement, the measurements being applied, and the time it will take to uncover the relevant trends.

What can be concluded from the final business case report?

The information in the report will define if there is a business case for a sales transformation from a financial perspective. It will define what top-line and bottom-line revenue can be achieved. The review will identify the intensity of the project, its resources, and the impact it will have on the operational side of the business along with the cultural element.

It is important to highlight, in the event of the review not finding sufficient validation for a project, that this is actually not a bad thing. This is confirming how well managed the sales organization is operating and demonstrating that maximum profit is being extracted through this area of the business. This can have many positive effects on those in the business and be a source of great motivation if managed correctly.

From this point the organization can make the decision about its next step.

Chapter 17:

Getting the Project Set Right

Completing a sales force transformation is a project that requires defined leadership, processes, priorities, and outcomes. The fortunate part of the sales force transformation is that the financial results can be seen early in the process and throughout, unlike other projects often undertaken by organizations.

A review must be completed that pinpoints each and every component that will form part of the sales transformation. This step alone is vital because if the contributing elements are not identified, large holes can be left in the process moving forward. I often see companies that have embarked on improvement programs for their sales forces and find that after several months, they have unbalanced their organizations more than they have improved them.

Getting the transformation team right

Depending on how the sales organization is currently structured (and how lean you are now operating for resources), you may elect to have the sales manager as the project leader or engage an assistant to the sales manager and executive team to work on some of the process. There are also companies where the executive team takes the role of the project leaders, overseeing the projects progress while the sales manager focuses on the team and the assistant on the task requirements.

At all times the sales manager will be the primary person in the project, as they are the person providing the direct coaching and guidance to the team and assisting the culture of the business in adopting the new practices that bring about sales force effectiveness. For a sales manager to do all aspects of the project on his or her own will be difficult due to the hours associated with completing the transformation.

Having an assistant, where resources allow it, is an ideal approach as you have someone who is focused on doing the behind-the-scenes tasks in preparation for use by the sales manager.

The person would be a full-time employee and someone with an understanding and passion for systems and effectiveness. He or she may have come from an administrative background with sales exposure and thus may understand some of the requirements and how to trace points through the business.

The project leader (sales manager) will be instrumental in how the project will flow and the impact that it will have on the organization. It is important the project leader have the ability to inform and engage others in the project and have them follow the structures and processes. It is also important this person can follow the structures and processes set down and within the timelines established.

Establishing the project priorities

When the reference of 'project' is applied to the transformation, it is using the universal reference to all activities that will occur in the overall project. Within that universal reference are a series of subprojects that will require management to achieve the outcomes. The order and priority of each of those subprojects is important and must be set in hierarchal order. You cannot start all subprojects simultaneously, as they will often clash in their requirements in implementation to the business. There will be a crossover in priorities for individual managers and team members, making the tasks unnecessarily difficult to complete.

The review process has identified all the tasks that need to be completed, and now the roadmap must be set down of what priorities need to be applied. It may be necessary to drill down and explore further into the requirements for the resolution of each of the points it identified. Each point may have a subproject and should be allocated with either a name or a number for reference by everyone.

Setting down the baseline

The baseline: what is actually happening in the business at this time? Has the current performance been tracked and documented so facts have been obtained in relation to the trends and processes that deliver the current outcomes? Do you know exactly what a change will, be both positive and negative, against the current baseline in the organization?

The subprojects need to be broken down into sizeable chunks that can be managed and improved. This is all about attention to details and not the thirty-thousand-foot or even the ten-thousand-foot view. The subprojects must be focused on specific points and have clear requirements within each subproject that people can follow easily. Where there are complications or misunderstandings, the subproject will freeze. When defining the project, each subproject can be a stopping point for the project that achieves a deliverable.

Treating the right issues

There will be a number of points that require careful analysis through cause-and-effect methodology to ensure you are addressing the right problems in the business. One of the reactions by most people that attempt to rush through a transformation is the treatment of effects rather than causes. This often will occur when companies are looking for fast or Band-Aid solutions to problems without giving full consideration to the ramifications of the intended changes. They are reacting to heightened problems that have reached a point of standing well out as problematic, rather than working proactively to explore the cause. If the priorities of the project are not right, often it can create new effects that people attempt to work on rather than looking back at what caused the issues in the first instance.

Avoiding false starts

Another challenge that can occur for project leaders is they are either excited about getting started on the implementation or being pushed by executives to commence the implementation. Some things will stand out and become total frustration to the business once the executives are aware of it from the review, and it's important not to engage in false starts. False starts are where you are commencing subprojects based on the "largest standout" or "highest frustration." Starting too early with insufficient information will stall the entire project, just as much as setting people about a series of tasks or subprojects before they are fully explored or viewed for the impact across other potential projects. The repercussions of what you are starting are not fully understood, and the organization may not be sufficiently educated to adapt to the project requirements.

Keeping the focus simultaneously on the top and bottom line

With all actions is it important to consider the top-line impact and bottom-line impact. There are as many opportunities in any organization to increase costs as there are to reduce costs. During the establishment of the project action points you need to consider, "Am I removing resources and processes that will enable a higher level of activity in the top line or creating process that will reduce the level of opportunity for the top line?"

The other challenge that can occur is that people get carried away with putting in too many processes, systems, and reports, making the organization dysfunctional. Work in any government office for a few weeks and you will see this firsthand!

The transformation project is not about throwing resources at problems, thinning companies out, or having tools to hold salespeople accountable by management.

The transformation project is about

- enabling the sales organization to secure more opportunities in a competitive market, delivering higher top-line revenue;

- streamlining internal processes to support their efforts, removing indirect costs and barriers;

- enabling the organization to be flexible to the market;

- providing management with information that allows for effective decision making;

- empowering salespeople to be more effective in the field;

- ensuring learning experiences from others, reducing their ramp-up time and effectiveness;

- allowing the collective intelligence of the organization provide the momentum to excel and not being reliant on one individual having the answers.

This is what the sales transformation is about, and each and every project affects not only the culture of the business but the top- and bottom-line profitability.

Creating the summary of all subprojects

Within the transformation, there will be subprojects of tasks that need to be completed. Each of the subprojects will stand in its own right as a viable project to be completed. This will be a work breakdown structured (WBS) process being applied. You then need to give consideration to what will happen when all projects are combined. It is like putting a jigsaw together. All the pieces seem alright on their own, but do they all fit together to make one correct picture at the end of the day? The complexity of the projects and subprojects and their impact within the organizations needs to be considered against other projects that may be operating or planned to be completed. The process should not be stopped due to other projects, but it may require re-prioritizing of the processes to gain the best outcomes.

Once all the subprojects have been scoped, a summary needs to be completed that will look at the realism of the entire project being delivered. Does it work in a seamless process across the business or are their clashes in time, resources, and priorities? This mapping process can be assisted by Gantt charts, which are covered in a later chapter on tools. A Gantt chart is a type of bar chart that illustrates a project schedule and shows the start and finish dates of the milestones and summary elements of a project. Ideally, as each subproject was developed it was scheduled to a Gantt chart to ensure that sufficient time allocation was applied. The Gantt chart will assist in establishing realistic timing for each of the subprojects and establishing an overall smooth flow.

You need to map out a resource chart and identify any potential challenges. Do you have sufficient resources? Are they scaled correctly so you are not over- or under-resourced in fluctuations throughout the project?

Another consideration is the number of tasks you are asking people to complete. This will impact the acceptance of change in the organization. The key to success is ideally giving people the confidence to commence the next subproject and complete it.

Putting your finger on the project "go" button

The summary of the projects is what the executive will be most interested in reviewing. On reporting to the executive, you should be able to confirm the following information prior commencement.

- Whether all subprojects been fully scoped, and the total number of subprojects to be managed

- What the planned outcomes are

- What the overall business impact is

- When the first results will be seen

- What timelines for the other results are

- What level of resources are required

- Whether the overall project is within budget

- What is the profit improvement outcome for the organization

By working through this process and defining the project, you have ensured that you know all the necessary details for the project to be operated effectively and achieve the desired outcome. The defining of the project is potentially a more important step than the actual business case. It is the final mapping and outline of the project and provides the detail and facts necessary for the project to operate. It has reviewed all potential barriers, crossovers, and opportunities, and the workflow to improve the operation of the business and reduction of the profit chasm.

From this point the project can move forward with confidence.

Chapter 18:

It's All About the Baseline

For the success of transforming to a high-performance, highly effective sales organization, you need to establish a baseline. What is the platform you will build from and what are the requirements of that platform? Without a clear baseline you will have very little to management guidelines, and the goalposts will keep changing according to the challenges you face from within and outside the business.

The executive way

The first and most important adjustment that has to happen is a potential change in attitude of executives and management on how sales forces are managed. Often I find that when you give executives more tools of transparency, they become immediately frustrated with what they are seeing in reports and processes in the early days of the transformation. That frustration must at no time be vented in such a way that the team feel criticized, victimized, or fearful of putting forward the information that is required in a more transparent and accountable organization.

I have seen this happen on many occasions when companies see the realities of what past management practices have created and look for instant changes in the team. You must remember it was the company that created everything that appears within new reporting disciplines and the company is wholly responsible. The decision was made or condoned at some point in time to operate a business that produced the results of the past. If the company is not comfortable with them when new methods of looking at the business are applied, then they need to work through those points steadily and guide the teams to where they need them to be now.

For the baseline to be successful and accepted by team members, the senior executive and sales manager must accept the responsibility of ensuring that the tools, processes, and systems are in place to support the success of each person. Without them, team members will see these baselines as threats, not as the support they are intended to be. Again, the balance of sales culture and sales force systems is imperative.

The baseline forms a foundation and understanding of the intention and focus of everyone in the sales organization. It gives a common meaning to performance requirements and the clarity of those standards. That clarity gives the sales team members an understanding of what is expected of them and sales managers the knowledge of what is required to support the sales team.

A new way of looking at measurement

As a priority, you need to measure the sales organization on the basis of the baseline opportunity and outcome, not historical performance as most organizations do. You need to know several things: What opportunity and how much opportunity exists for the sales organization? What is the best approach to secure that opportunity? What is a realistic timeline within which it can be achieved? Is that opportunity based on the current market or new markets? Taking those opportunities into consideration, what is the likely outcome of that effort? Most importantly, you need to know in detail how much effort is required to secure that opportunity in behaviors and performance requirements.

If the organization is unable to clearly establish what realistic growth is and articulate the detailed path (in writing) for the sales team members, then they cannot drive the salespeople to perform their tasks. Clarity of where the opportunity is and the degree of effort required, without assumptions from industry backgrounds and experience, is a major motivator and clear path for sales individuals to follow.

The baseline stumbling blocks

In many of the companies I review that are preparing to embark on the transformation, I find growth potential is one element that is only partially done. Some companies have a good understanding of their markets and opportunities but fail to understand the effort and moneymaking line to operate the salespeople on underpinning it. It is not something that is taught in most sales management courses and certainly not something that comes from university. It is grounded in experience and knowledge, based on the turnarounds I completed where immediate results were required. When you take that same methodology and apply it to a transformation, you have consistent, measureable growth delivered.

Another important baseline is "near enough is not good enough." This is something I talk a lot about in seminars as people place relationships with teams over results. You can manage both simultaneously as long as you have right management tools and disciplines in place. In some countries, an organization's budgets or sales goalsquota are based on the organization setting a target figure—the amount the sales force should aim for—rather than the minimum performance requirement of the team. Therefore, when an organization reaches the end of its financial year and finds its sales team has made 95 percent of the sales goals/budget, it is usually very pleased with itself—95 percent success isn't as good as exceeding budget/ sales goals, but it's not that far off, either. Now some people reading this would be saying, "surely this is not true"; but different countries and industries have different views of what is good and acceptable. Some organizations may even celebrate the outcome as a good year—a celebration of a baseline that "near enough is good enough."

By contrast, an organization espousing to be a high-performance and effective sales organization would look at the missing 5 percent and ask, "Why didn't we make it?" Near enough is most definitely not good enough. The new sales organization is all about being achievers and aiming to be well over budget/quota each year.

This next baseline is embedded heavily with the requirement for the organization to know what it is doing and how to assist sales individuals to be over budget/quota. If the organization has a record of underperformance and cannot plan the path, in detail, of how to perform to this level of requirement, then it cannot use this measurement philosophy on the team. It is the core of what a leader is coaching and guiding the team to fulfill. Leadership is required to have articulated this in advance so it's a proven or well-documented path forward that is logical and easily followed. The risk should be reviewed and managed before the team leaves the office.

The next baseline is that of structure and processes. For success in your organization, and to reinforce the baseline outlined above, you need to have in place very clear organization lines of management with clear boundaries. People need clarity about their roles: clear boundaries and measurements defining the exact nature and level of the performance you require of each contributor to the team—what is acceptable and what is unacceptable.

The clarity of those boundaries produces results for the future. They should know what tasks they can do, what they cannot do, and how to perform each component of their roles.

This baseline is where the sales manager must accept responsibility for the development of the tools and systems that will support the team. The quality of those systems and tools is imperative to the success of the team. Where they leave gaps and lack of information, this will directly equate to teams underperforming.

Getting structure and process right

The baseline of structure and processes encompasses the quality of all operational requirements and procedure requirements, reporting processes and coaching. Many traditional sales managers cringe at the thought of discipline, systems, and processes to the required level, but that is how successful businesses operate. That is the winning edge new sales managers have over their older counterparts.

Often you will find there are some fragments of the requirements lost somewhere in the intranet that commonly form templates for proposals and related items. Most have been altered so many times the originals cannot be recognized. The filing system has things located everywhere with a myriad of file names; in effect, there is no filing system. The version control went out the window when three salespeople were given the opportunity to change templates for each task they undertook.

Often organizations appoint a product manager to lead the team on specific information regarding individual products or product groups. Where a product manager is in place, the person must be managed in such away that at all times they are building a documented resource base of knowledge that is available to salespeople on demand.

Large corporations have deep resources and invest in having documented and in-depth knowledge bases with details of product capability and selling requirements for each of those products, to ensure that the knowledge gained by the product manager is accessible and shared across all sales individuals. It is not possible for one individual product manager to service all the needs of all salespeople's inquiries within the business, hence the base is set up to minimize their workload.

Those larger companies have learned that one person cannot share sufficient information across a team of salespeople verbally or on demand to have them effectively operate in the market.

The curse of the product manager

In many of the smaller companies I review, I see them support a practice where the product manager is an integral part of the sales effort and very hands-on with every sales individual. This person carries his or her knowledge in the head with limited documentation, much like how the salespeople operate with customer knowledge. A product manager or others with specific product knowledge who are not documenting the information into a transferrable resource situation are placing unnecessary barriers in front of sales individuals and increasing indirect costs to the company.

Structure and systems show the way to make money

Commonly people assume that more systems make it the harder to manage teams. This is a myth and one that was potentially started by a person who was anti-systems. Systems make communication easier for everyone in an organization. They reduce the time required to communicate information multiple times by individuals when it should be just operational process. They show people exactly how to operate on the moneymaking line.

The cost of operating a business based on verbal communication versus structure and systems is considerably higher. You are taking a high-cost resource to repeat the conversation over and over that could be obtainable in a fraction of the time—easy to access, clear in content, and fast for delivery.

Yes there is a cost in setting all this up, but it is minuscule in comparison to the cost of verbal processes. Interestingly, where no systems, processes, and tools are in place, management will spend more than 50 percent of its time on managing the lower-scale elements of a sales individual's role. It is like attempting to manage a field of football players by standing in the grandstand yelling, hoping they hear you as they run around everywhere doing what they believe is right.

Building to world-class standards rather than our-class standards

A key component of the transformation is to be building a world-class sales organization rather than our-class. Our-class means documenting what the company already does rather than installing what is required to meet the standards of world-class. You cannot improve performance by documenting only what you have done in the past. There will be elements that are retained, but you must be aiming for world-class at all times. New knowledge must be contributed that refines processes and improves standards in all aspects of the sales organization.

Well-documented processes ensure that there is never any misunderstanding of requirements and standards for each role. Everyone must know and agree on what is expected of them. These are all the resources and proven processes that will ensure each sales individual excels in his or her role.

Giving it a makeover and making money

I was once engaged on an assignment with a well-known cosmetics company to drive the sales results. On initial review of the business, it seemed they were well set with human resource documentation, quality assurance, and general operational processes, and their understanding was that this was sufficient to operate the team. The teams were all underperforming for a number of reasons, most of which could be traced back to the two issues: poor recruitment and poor management.

I immediately installed the new sales force systems, standards, reporting, management processes; and all requirements of sales force effectiveness. The business regained its year-to-date losses in week eight of the assignment, was over budget at week twelve, and grew in excess of 110 percent in under ten months. The new acquisition customer levels broke all records and customers were managed for lifetime value, with repeat sales increasing to levels never seen in the organizations in the past.

Interestingly, poor-performing sales individuals marked by the management for departure, in the new environment changed to be top performers once they had the clarity and boundaries of what their role requirements were. They also reported back to the organization's directors that the clarity had motivated them and made the difference in how they operated as salespeople in the field.

They understood and accepted the baseline and were willing to work within that structure. This is not an isolated incident and has been reported across many other organizations.

We learned to fail many times over and over

If you view this baseline from another perspective, you are allowing the salespeople to go to market and experiment at your organization's expense. When untrained newcomers are thrown out there in the field, they are likely to bumble in front of customers and present images of institutional incompetence. They may walk past any number of opportunities as they are not trained or experienced enough to identify them.

What is being allowed to happen here is to let them go on making the same mistakes others learned to avoid years ago, and to wander around in all directions in the hope of finding the path to success. Each time a beginner reinvents the wheel at your organization's expense, it costs the organization directly in terms of financial loss and opportunity loss.

Sales Focus International calculated the potential loss in taking this approach versus a more structured approach, through the ramp-up times for sales individuals from hiring to consistently achieving budget/quota. The difference is 60 percent less revenue through the learning phase. Usually the ramp-up or learning phase is double the timeline when someone is using their own business approach.

When you transform a sales organization, you are not just focusing on people and processes—it is all about profit. A transformation must put results in the top and bottom line if it is designed and delivered correctly.

Chapter 19:
Managing the High-Performance Sales Team

Managing a high-performance sales team is not an easy task. You cannot just sit back, turn on the engine, and point to where you want to go and it will glide down the road delivering results. It has to be driven like a car, making minor adjustments all the time to get to the desired destination. Even with a GPS unit on board giving you all the data, you still need to make decisions and guide it in the right direction.

Great sales teams work for great managers. Bad sales teams work for underperforming sales managers. Great sellers do not work for bad companies. Bad sellers do not work for great companies. As harsh as that may sound—it's a fact of life.

Getting your license to drive

A sales team can only be as good as the manager who leads it, and it's that manager's role to create the high-performance team. It will not just happen by chance and can often prove to be an arduous task, as a sales manager must encourage both competitive behavior and a results-driven work ethic, while keeping the sales team focused on delivering to agreed plans and strategies. When achieving this fine balance, a sales manager will be able to boost the team's performance, increase profitability, and gain competitive advantage.

To effectively manage a team, it is important that you measure the right indicators that will tell you what needs to be driven, what needs to be improved, and what is working well for you. Without the measurement, you are just guessing what needs to be done. There is no room for a gut feeling or fast-changing decisions to counteract poor decisions when you are leading a team of people that are responsible for the top-line revenue of any organization.

Measurement does not improve performance

One of the myths I encounter frequently with executives is the notion that measurement improves performance. They feel that by putting in measurements, the results will naturally happen. The transparency will give the understanding of how to perform better, so sales must go up.

Measuring the right things is clearly important, and measuring the right things often suggests the appropriate course of action to make genuine improvement. But measurement alone isn't enough, and many people don't change their behavior even when the obvious is right in front of them. Habits are stronger motivators than measurements.

Every organization you know of measures sales on a monthly or quarterly basis. Every organization measures and reports on profits. But not every organization sees its sales or its profits rise every quarter. Many companies have pipelines or sales funnels they operate, but again, sales do not naturally rise with the information at hand.

The effort to develop a world-class sales organization cannot start and stop with measurement, although you need quality information and measurement to support the development of a high-performance team or a world-class sales organization.

What we do know from all the organizations I have reviewed is that there is typically a lack of measurement in relation to the sales organization being utilized, and the organization is often operating with its hands tied behind its back, hoping it can break through the sales goal/budget barrier each measured period.

Measurement assists in good decision making and people's actions

Measurement is about having sufficient information to make informed decisions. It is about measuring the right thing for your organization that will assist in the strategy being successfully implemented. The measurement provides historical, current, and predictive views of the sales operation through reporting. It allows you to make more intelligent decisions.

Good measurement takes you from being a manager of process, to being a leader—someone who can accurately predict the future trends and consistently make good decisions.

Many organizations are overly reliant on the executive-level data of revenue and profit and lack enough depth on the key metrics that drive their business units. Where the measurement breaks down the processes and measures contributing elements rather than outcome, a more informed understanding leads to more informed decisions. Decisions are made on the causes of problems rather than the effects. The number that needs to be applied is entirely dependent on the complexity of the business.

Good managers make good decisions

Good managers can then make decisions of what they need to change, improve, or remove in relation to finite steps within all the processes. This alerts them to changing market conditions well in advance. It provides them with the immediate knowledge of coaching requirements or new tools required for salespeople to take to market.

A great sales organization makes many small and minor adjustments through the weeks/months and keeps travelling in the right direction at all times. They do allow the team to go off track and turn down the wrong road and then have to make major adjustments to bring them back on track. There are no knee-jerk reactions to the market; they watch the trends and understand how situations are evolving.

They provide sales teams with confidence and good leadership, as they are great decision makers.

It is important that the measurement does not appear in screeds of pages of information. It should be a single-page report and dashboard that quickly identifies the trends and behaviors of the sales organization against the sales plan. A key point is that if you are not measuring to a plan that is sufficiently detailed and demonstrates that precise moneymaking line, then you are wasting your time.

In my experience this information can take an organization that is relatively inexperienced as a sales organization to an informed and strong-selling organization within months, as long as the right plan is in place.

It empowers managers to make the right decisions to drive their personnel in the right direction, and it provides them with the detailed information that directs them to precisely where the sales individuals require coaching and guiding.

To be a good manager and manage a high-performance sales organization, the most important skill you must have is to be a good decision maker. You will be judged every day on your decisions and you cannot leave this to risk. It is the move from being just a people manager to a commercial manager.

Managers operating on hearsay and next to no systems will often convince themselves they are right, often based on gut feelings. They communicate with people who support their opinions of what is happening in the market and, as pressure builds on sales results, they recruit even more people to their cause of supporting their opinions–whether they are customers, fellow sales personnel, or vendors.

Although the information is subjective, major decisions will be made, as the person giving such support is perceived as reliable. Do these managers purposefully mislead the business? Definitely not. They are just seeking refuge in hearsay rather than facing facts that can challenge their beliefs and conduct. A number of important ingredients go into good decision making:

- A good decision will come only from fact and never from hearsay. Always review your situation and make sure you are responding to the facts.

- A good decision will be based on an equal balance of future financial performance, trends, and business intelligence, combined with past financial performance.

- A good decision maker will take some calculated risks that can expose you as wise or incompetent in your role. Decision makers do not make foolhardy decisions, but they do take risks that are calculated and experience-based. Business intelligence for the sales organization reduces the exposure to poor or incompetent decisions.

- A good decision maker will not panic or offer a justification for failure if a bad or poor decision is made. You can always review the business intelligence to see how you arrived at that decision and learn from what was overlooked. The focus must be not so much on the decision you just made as on how quickly you analyze the situation and act with a response that involves a better decision to rectify the situation. You will then be judged less on the poor decision and more on how you acknowledged it and remedied it.

If a decision maker has a track record of bad decisions, there is a form of forgiveness that will not apply. Forgiveness wears thin. In business you are constantly making decisions with sales forces. They can range from small decisions to major decisions on a day-to-day basis. You are dealing with a moving and often volatile situation, as sales individuals are influenced by the market, customers, and your own organization.

As a manager of a sales organization, you are always being asked, for example, whether particular customers can be given some sort of benefit or discount, whether there can be a change to their terms, what to charge them in specific situations, or whether a salesperson should attend a location—the list goes on. If you have no systems, in fact, your day will be spent answering those questions, believing that is a manager's primary function. Combined with those smaller, day-to-day decisions are questions that will affect the business in a more significant way. These will be questions regarding how a salesperson approaches certain customers, what information should be in proposals, and, whether product lines should be focused upon. Again it will depend on the maturity of your systems.

Then there are the really major decisions—such as business strategy, product mix, marketing content, and human resources-related decisions. The list is endless and will be dependent on your business operation and product/services. Good measurement will assist you in those decisions and, more importantly, provide immediate feedback on whether those decisions were sound or require revisiting. It will also show you ways to quickly revisit them. It will keep you on the pulse of the business, rather than constantly reviewing what happened in the past through traditional reporting methods.

If you are taking the team through a transformation project from being an average sales organization to the most effective sales organization, you will not achieve this unless you have in place the right information.

High-performance teams do not just happen. They are built from focused strategies that are broken down to individual requirements. The individuals are supported with the right systems and tools to perform their roles. They are managed through facts and consistent coaching of the right information to support and improve their behaviors and performance.

They are managed by a good decision maker, and most importantly the team is rewarded for efforts, ranging from a pat on the back at the moment of achievement through to major awards.

Chapter 20:
The New Customer Dilemma

Imagine you have a dilemma where you have the opportunity and capacity to secure a lot of new customers (often referred to as new business). You just require the right people in the right roles to make it happen. When an organization is aligned to world-class methodologies, they find this dilemma presents itself to potentially a much greater degree than in the past. It becomes a core requirement within the business to fulfill the capacity and maximize the sales results being delivered by the sales force.

The acquisition of new customers is an ongoing requirement for the longevity of any organization. It can be the catalyst for significant growth and is the most cost-effective way to expand a business when done correctly. New business is the replacement mechanism for existing customers that are lost through natural attrition in the market.

Taking the acid test

Most importantly, signing new customers demonstrates the true talent of any sales organization—its ability to secure new customers and be directly measured against competitors. The greater the value of those new accounts and the frequency in which they are signed demonstrates the greater skill of the sales organization. I often refer to this new customers signing as the acid test of any salesperson.

A salesperson who cannot sign reasonable-sized new accounts is not worth having on a team. It is a skill that demonstrates a salesperson's true capability in selling to be able to target and secure the business. It requires a combination of business acumen, planning, research, selling capability, and development of businesses cases or reasons for the target customer to change vendors. All those skills are needed in variation to up-sell and cross-sell within existing accounts effectively. You cannot be a good account manager if you do not have those skills also, so there is no delineation between new business sellers and existing account managers in a high-performance sales organization.

For many years salespeople have enjoyed good times in the market, and many have not been required to acquire new customers with any frequency. The natural momentum of the market gave them a starting point that can only be remembered as history now in the new world. Many salespeople in today's market have never sold in tough times and don't understand the skill requirements that need to be applied.

The redundant seller

In the past, salespeople have been nominated as being account managers, farmers, client managers, and every other title that invites the person to serve only existing customers. Their customer accounts grew through the natural growth of their customers and with very little contribution from the seller. They operated in an environment where most of the work has been done already; they just needed to keep the customer informed, the organization delivered what the customer wanted, and business kept rolling in.

This is the majority of sellers that are available in the market today and the group that presents itself when hiring. There is a small group of individuals that are the good sellers that can sign new business, drive growth in accounts, and be strong contributors to the top- and bottom-line revenue. For every good seller you will probably meet about one hundred-plus of the ordinary sellers.

With the shift in the market in the last few years, many salespeople from the average skills pool of people is increasing rapidly. The level of movement on résumés from 2008 onward is staggering and if you know the industries, companies, and customer bases they sell to, you can quickly see who was in the first cut of poor performers, second cut, etc. The problem that all sales managers and salespeople face now is that a salesperson who cannot sign new customers is really just an order taker and of little value in today's new world after the global financial crisis. The new market has made sellers with no new customer-acquisition skills redundant; it's just a question of how long the employers will carry them. This is a growing pool of salespeople looking for work because they do not address this fundamental flaw in their skill sets.

These people are not your vehicle to success in a world-class sales organization.

With the implementation of world-class standards, you will need sellers that can sign new business and retain existing customers (skills within one person, not two people). The capacity-planning processes will demonstrate how far you can grow and how quickly, and the need for new business customers is always greater than the market's traditional growth levels. The rule of thumb is that rapid growth comes from new customer acquisition. Average growth comes from existing customers.

Business advisors often say that it is much cheaper to retain existing customers than to acquire new customers. This can be true, but it depends on the quality of sales efforts in attracting new customers and on how much marketing and other effort is involved in sustaining existing customers. It cannot be measured on just sales individuals' effort alone. It also does not calibrate the level of growth you wish to achieve with the organization.

What we do know is that if you do not keep bringing new customers into the business, it will inevitably contract as a result of existing customers changing, acquisitions ,and other marketplace influences that will eat away at your revenues. In the global recession, people have experienced drops of up to 40 percent in revenue as their existing customer bases vanished. No company can survive in that environment without a strong focus on new customer acquisition.

Are you learning on borrowed time

The organizations that will struggle the most now will be the ones that are coming from a base of "no new customers" practices and experience and are attempting to hone their skills in one of the toughest markets seen in many years. Many sales managers will also be confronted with the reality that their skill sets require immediate attention in new business acquisition as their mantra and actions for the past decade has been customer relationships and existing accounts.

Those companies that were focused on existing accounts are learning the basics of how to do new business, while other companies have matured capabilities that will stifle any attempts to compete against them.

Hence you start to see industries being plagued with price-cutting and other non-sensible offerings in the market in an attempt to lure the customers their way. They are compensating for the lack of skill in the team through loss of profits.

The focus must be in establishing the skills and requirements for salespeople (and some sales managers) to sell new customers for your organization. This has to be done quickly and with strong coaching of individuals to ensure that the number of opportunities lost is minimized.

Another dilemma you face: you must also appreciate that if your organization is not good in the area of selling new customers, you will most unlikely hire someone that is. People that are strong new customer sellers can quickly ascertain a potential employer's capability in this area and whether the right support tools and resources are in place to support their efforts. Where they find gaps, they do not become your employees. Good new business sellers do not fall for the opportunity of going out there and carving a new path for the company. Only young, blind individuals that do not understand how hard the journey is take on such a project.

There are many things that contribute to the success of a salesperson in the signing of new customers—including the offering being made and its relevance to the market; their attitude, savvy, and skill level; the tools provided to help them sign the business; and the tenacity to stick with it— to name a few. A world-class sales organization has all those ingredients in place.

Hiring? - then bear this in mind

When hiring sellers, you have to carefully scrutinize their experience and expectations of how they will bring in new business and the timelines in their minds. Remember, their belief is their reality and you need to understand their reality. This is best understood through an example of an interview I was doing recently for a client.

The client was in an industry that had taken a strong hit in the market, and new business sellers were critical to his future. I was asked to do short-list interviews to assist him in finding the right person. He presented this person as a good-quality candidate from a recruitment agency.

When interviewing, I listen very closely to statements made by salespeople about their thoughts on how they will perform specific tasks.

Invest in me, he says

The gentleman was asked to outline his approach to new customers. He mentioned building relationships and networking. (At that point I knew we were sitting with the wrong candidate, but the client needed to learn how to extrapolate the right information.) I asked him to outline his strategy to securing new business if I provided him with a list of target accounts to approach. Immediately he again went back to talking about relationships. Realizing his skills were not going to yield much information outside of basic answers, I then asked what his experience was in timelines for securing new customers. He informed us that it was about six to nine months, but could be longer depending on whom he was targeting. I then remarked that if his role required a high level of new customers, it would be some time until any results would be seen. His response to this was that was hiring him was an investment and the company should invest in him during that period of time and he would return the results. The interview was carried on a little further and then politely closed.

What this applicant forgot was that when you invest in anything, you look for performance of the investment previously to ascertain the potential in the future. Being unable to demonstrate new customer acquisition skills outside of relationships and networking made him a poor investment. If he had outlined his method of targeting, research, strategy, competitor analysis, decision-maker exploration, and problem identification, then he would have been a good investment.

You can wonder why he was presented as a good candidate initially. The interesting thing about this man was that his resume would have impressed anyone from the industry. He had worked at good organizations for three to four years in each role. His career was rising and he said all the right things in writing, but alas he was better at preparing résumés than actually selling.

Needless to say, our client elected to provide him the opportunity to work for a competitor where he would provide the least amount of resistance for his company in acquiring the business.

As an executive, you have to accept that in today's world there are only a limited number of top professional sellers, and the employers vying to hire those sellers are limitless. In a recent presentation to some two hundred and fifty executives I asked, "Can you please raise your hand if you are open to hiring a really top seller who can sign new customers consistently?" As I looked across the room, there were over two hundred and fifty hands in the air. Some put up two hands in an attempt to stand out from the crowd and emphasize their desire for a top seller!

The realities of life now are you must realize and accept that, for most organizations, sales teams will start out being a combination of average-skilled people. The team will be more comfortable with existing customers than with new customers, and strong management will be needed to keep it focused and performing beyond traditional levels.

When your organization makes the shift to being a high-performance sales organization, the dynamics change considerably. The team that was once average performers is guided to be great performers. You don't go out and hire a new team of top performers; you build them from your existing team.

The making of legends

In high-performance teams, the management style is about leadership, coaching, guiding, and creating great sellers. It is about having the right tools and the right alignment to the market and setting people up to be highly successful. Provide the guidance and support on a daily/weekly/monthly basis to ensure they excel and in turn, the sales organization excels. It goes back to the difference between the junior high school sports game and the professional-league game mentioned earlier in the book.

The sales organization creates top sellers that secure new business consistently and drive significant top-line and bottom-line growth.

Chapter 21:

Does the Transformation Affect the Wider Organization?

The question is, "Can you change one part of the organization without it affecting the other areas?"

Most organizations are continually unbalanced, based on the approach to improvement they are taking. The focus is often placed on one area or business unit for improvement at a time and this is continually putting the business off balance. Some elements of a business can be improved without impact across the wider organization, but most have some direct or indirect impact. If you consider that when you improve the production capacity of a production line by say 30 percent, then that capacity has to be sold, so the sales organization and its budgets are immediately affected.

One step at time can create one mountain at a time

When you change a business unit and don't look at the wider organizational impact, it can create a culture of "us versus them" between business units as the focus shifts across the company. The changes are reactionary to issues rather than strategic growth phases in all areas of the business.

In many organizations, changes are made with little real consideration to the impact in other areas and the ability of those areas to respond to the changing dynamics within the organization. People are suffocated from innovation and they become focused on employment stability rather than growth in the company. They become survivors within the organization rather than contributors.

What you will see is management operating from a hub, with individual focus on business units of the business. They may work on fixing say the finance area, leaving other areas to continue as done in the past. Then they shift their focus to another business unit, leaving the others to continue on. They are operating the business in units rather than as an organization with a wider community. The organization becomes unbalanced as the weight of focus moves across each of the business units.

It is like tipping the scale. This has a direct impact on the bottom line and dilutes people's ability to see the vision of the organization and adopt the right behaviors.

The balanced organization

The balanced organization is focused on development consistently across the business without limitation to a specific business unit. The development is based on a strong understanding of the impact across other business units and a high level of communication and foresight in the management teams to predict and guide the organization through the changes with the least amount of barriers placed in front of it.

Each business unit is responsible for the impact within its area of responsibility and what the requirements are to improve. The culture is developed of a team versus individual focus, as people are aware that everyone must equally contribute to the improvement and not be reliant on everyone else changing except them. When this approach is taken, you have a balanced organization.

The most critical element to create a balanced organization is the communication channels. In most organizations the communication by team members is across the company, providing the management with little knowledge or incorrectly filtered knowledge of what is occurring at the front line of its area of responsibility. A good common example is salespeople approaching various individuals within the production or logistics areas in the pursuit of customer order status. The operational side of the business can have some twenty contact hits a day from various sales individuals. In some companies I have seen this escalate to the point where operations considered hiring an administration person just to answer salespeople's internal questions.

When you are making changes within the organization, it can easily unbalance existing processes with no direct means of measurement and development to restabilize them. The repercussions across the business are not identified, only the impact within a specific business unit. The other business units suffer at the hand of other units' changes.

This is commonly attributed to a lack of structured communication between each of the business unit leaders.

Conversations are limited to how they are performing rather than how they are improving. When companies operate with this lower-ranks cross communication, they have little opportunity for editing and applying a management process for continual improvement. They experience lower productivity and a high level of duplication of tasks and processes, and the organization has a higher cost to function.

When you have the right quality of conversation between unit managers, you have improvement communication that can contribute to the reduction of costs and duplications. The business is in a state of continuous improvement.

Cross communication creates cross employees

Where processes are employed that provide management with the opportunity of continual editing and continual improvement, the organization rapidly improves its productivity. Cross communication within the lower ranks occurs only within the set guidelines and structures to increase productivity and minimize the level of duplication of tasks and processes. Managers are drawing the right information they need from other areas to remove the duplications and causes of lower productivity, and taking action on it.

For the sales organization to become world-class, the executive must be focused on improvement across a number of business units and not follow traditional business practices of focusing on the firefighting issue or obvious cost-cutting. The sales organization does directly impact other areas and often creates the entire culture of the business. A chaotic and randomly operating sales organization creates a chaotic and random larger organization as the company responds to the customer demands and actions promised by sales.

Good communication supports good transformations

The key to the implementation of a world-class sales organization is the communication between other business unit leaders to understand the impact on their units, the improvements that can be made, and the removal of duplicated tasks, reworking of tasks, and all the other indirect cost functions that occur in a business. People are focused on the right tasks with the right information to allow the organization to grow.

The organization must be prepared for growth and have the processes in place to take action on the right things that stop the traditional barriers created in cause and effect.

In many of the turnaround assignments I have delivered, I have discussed with executives the need for the other areas of the business to be attuned to what is happening. The executive's responsibility is to keep communication alive and work on improvement as the dynamics and results of the sales organization change. Some take heed of the advice and embark on setting up the processes and meeting content, etc.

Other executives see sales as a division (the wording being an apt point) and just want sales increased. They need cash flow and profit to improve their situation and believe the rest of the organization can function perfectly if the sales revenue is coming through the door. To a point that is correct, but there is a tipping point where sales are good and then sales become the corruption point of the organization.

The unbalanced organization implosion

I remember one company in particular who was involved in production. Its turnover was around $10 million per annum so it had grown to a point where lessons were learned and some smarts had been put in the business. They were baffled by the sales force, and the sales manager was unable to lead the team. They had a good product and story to take to market, just the wrong people in the wrong roles and a team that had learned to play games. We took over the management of the team for a 120-day contract which included installing a new manager. The executive had no intention of changing anything else in the business and just wanted sales. The focus was on sales today and this month, mainly due to their cash flow issues.

The sales revenue immediately started to climb under new management and within 90 days had increased by some 40 percent. The pipeline of the business and information that was being tracked demonstrated that the business was on track for an 80 percent growth impact over the following twelve months based on tender conversions. The business was involved in the construction industry. The executives were relieved by the growth and the immediate cash flow issues being dissolved.

However, about two months later they called an emergency meeting as they had cash flow issues once again. They were experiencing too much growth and had failed to forecast correctly in relation to raw materials (imported from overseas), production capacity, and cash flow requirements to fulfill orders. We set them up with another organization that specialized in operational dysfunctionality. The company today is a very successful organization returning excellent profits.

When an organization embarks on being a world-class sales organizations, the executives need to engage with the other internal executives and business units to ensure that the company remains balanced and the indirect costs do not escalate out of control. The executive must assist in guiding the organization through the change and ensure that the culture is one of innovation and excellence in all business units, not just one.

Chapter 22:

Train to Achieve the Gain

As you will have discovered through reading this book and through your own experience, the success of any sales organization hinges on the skill of the individuals within the sales force—that of the managers or the people on the front line with the customers. Each person must be highly skilled in performing his or her role so the results can be delivered.

An organization must consistently invest in training its sales organization if it wants to see a change in the sales culture and improved performance. The training is not only about developing selling skills but is also responsible for creating a common language for the sales organization members and the behaviors required by them in the field or as support personnel. It supports the implementation of the strategic plan at the customer interface.

Who is likely to fail first

Managing sales forces requires many new skills as people shift from being people managers to commercial managers with people skills. In the past, the least amount of attention has been given to up-skilling of the sales managers, and often they are believed to just naturally have the talent. They are often selected for being good with people and everyone gets along with them. They are dedicated to the customers and know your industry and business, so therefore they must be good sales managers. They may have attended a basic program for how to manage teams, but the dust is so thick on the folder that it is unrecognizable and very little has been installed in the business as the company continued to do what it had always done.

Interestingly, Chally Group found in its research that 85 percent of top sellers fail in the role of sales manager in their first year. Their motivations of being a seller do not translate to being a good sales manager, yet they are the first pick of the company for hiring.

Kurlan Consulting (USA) research on sales managers found that

- 18 percent should not even be sales managers.
- 34 percent cannot be trained or coached to be sales managers.
- sales managers spend less than 15 percent of their time coaching their teams.
- only 7 percent of the population of sales managers are elite managers.

The perception of sales management being "good guys" is very dated and a high risk to any organization in the future. Sales managers must have commercial skills that ensure business practices are installed, and they must have people management skills.

The interesting quandary to all this is that there are many vendors across the world delivering sales management training for many years, so it begs the question: who is actually attending the training?

At a conference to senior executives, the following statement was made:

> *"The development of sales leaders is not a "nice to do," but rather a "must do." If we don't invest in ensuring that sales leadership teams, from first-line sales managers up to the top sales executive, have the skills and support services in place to make them as effective as possible, we will be hard-pressed for them to get the top performance from the teams under them."*

Kenneth R. Powell . Vice President of World-Wide Sales Enablement at Automatic Data Processing (ADP). Kenneth has some 4000 sales consultants in his organization and numerous levels of sales management.

The statement is conclusive.

Improvement comes from individuals improving too

As with sales individuals, if managers are not willing and demonstrating actions to improve, then the sales organization will not improve. Executives must provide them with the opportunities and encourage their participation in more advanced education.

The education and development should be ongoing to allow them to excel in their roles and in the organization. It is the organization's responsibility to develop its managers and leaders. Its only question must be, does the person have the attitude to want to learn and improve? If they do then the learning must begin. If they don't, then we will leave that answer up to you.

Training is and will always be the pivotal point between average and high-performance teams, the quality of training and delivery method being a vital point. If you consider the information covered in the levels of organizations, the difference between level one and level four is the degree of training or coaching. The team being coached daily is best placed to achieve; the team being coached with the right information every day, week, month, and year is the winner.

Here are some facts from accumulated research on training. The subject is extensively researched by chief learning officers, with many research papers are available through their literature.

- Training programs only account for 10 percent of changed performance on the job.

- Training in a formal setting accounts for 20 percent of a salesperson's learning; the balance of 80 percent is informal, meaning sales-manager driven.

- Training fails to transfer initially by up to 38 percent, and this percentage increases post training.

- Training in real-world situations directly relates to the quality of the overall training experience and knowledge transferred.

Front and center to success

The sales manager will be the pivotal person in the skill of the sales individuals and the overall development of the culture of the team. The sales manager will need to develop a sound plan for the training of all individuals in the team to ensure that everyone is appropriately skilled for the tasks they will be asked to do. Executives must also support that investment and understand that it is pivotal to the success of the sales organization.

For some countries and sales managers, this will be a major cultural change as they are not accustomed to training teams outside of the annual conference session. For other countries and sales managers, they will be shocked to read that companies don't train their teams religiously to ensure top performance. It is all about the culture of what you are used to and what you need to be doing.

Reinforcement of training sessions is critical to the success of the team. In order for that to happen, it's imperative that managers understand how to reinforce what was learned and how to use that learning to meet the goals of the sales organization. Failure to do so will lead to failed results. Why? Because the lessons, ideas, and skills learned in training are of little value if managers and executives fail to reinforce the training on an ongoing basis. When this happens, most salespeople either forget or ignore what they learned within a few hours or days; the potential for meaningful results is lost.

I remember that when I was doing three-day classroom-training public programs back in the 1990s, we had a process where we invited sales managers to attend free of charge; or for those who declared they were too busy, they could attend the final half-day session. The point was to connect the training to the field and the sales manager to reinforce the training. The results were that only one in ten managers ever attended the three full days. Only two in ten managers arrived for the final half day where people presented their plans. The rest saw no value in attending and commonly their sales teams were the least skilled in the room. We knew they were going back to same old same old under the stewardship of the sales manager.

We now operate the online training with all managers receiving the homework answers on each module for each person, and the engagement level now is over 90 percent with high reinforcement levels. We are unsure if it was a time issue or if sales managers have realized they need to be involved to get the value.

The responsibility falls to the manager to provide the reinforcement training and should have only limited ongoing requirements from the original trainer.

The support tools the training vendor leaves with the manager are the most imperative element. The sales manager must be enabled to deliver the reinforcement as the sales coach. An organization relying on the involvement of the sales trainer in an ongoing long-term arrangement is abdicating their responsibility as sales leader.

Why buy a dog and then bark too

There was a trend for many years where sales trainers would go in the field with sales individuals and do field training with them. They would attend customer visits and provide skills guidance. In my opinion this was the greatest abdication of sales management responsibility I had ever heard of, and a résumé of such an individual would be filed immediately in the circular file on the floor. This was a good marketing move from the sales-training companies, capitalizing on the laziness and incompetence of sales managers, but their focus should have been to train the sales manager. If the sales manager rejected the training then the CEO should have made the necessary decision. Managing people is about coaching and guiding people to deliver the outcomes on a daily, weekly, and monthly basis.

Effective coaching techniques should be transferred from the trainer to the manager, if the manager is not experienced in coaching. You must ensure that the manager is focused on how to coach rather than on telling people what to do. The coaching becomes part of the communication process, with the team guiding them on how to perform in their roles.

Nothing will be achieved without the training of every individual—including the sales manager—in the sales organization. If you are dedicated to creating a high-performance team, that is the most effective approach in the world.

Chapter 23:

What Will Ensure a Successful Transformation?

This is the question that CEOs ask. And often when they have made their minds up to shift the business to a new level, yesterday is when they wanted the results. They are aware of the losses being incurred and they want them resolved immediately. The "rush-in" approach is the one that will fail every business and cause more damage than good. Sales force transformation is a project and not a moment in time or great thing to use as vision with no substance.

For any project to be successful, there must be timelines established for accomplishments. There are a number of factors that need to be considered before setting down those timelines.

As many of you will have experienced to some degree, when you raise the subject of undertaking transformations or change (change management) in an organization, it has mixed reactions. Change management often can be a term that excites those leaders that are to deliver it and puts fear in the hearts of all those around them. Change means doing things differently, and that brings about the need for people to move out of their comfort zones to new ones. They don't know if the new practices will be more comfortable, but they are mostly content in keeping things the way they used to be. The words of "change management" are to some companies as toxic as saying "unemployment." The crisis has certainly escalated those words to more of a negative connation than a positive one.

Transformation versus change

When we use the terminology of "transformation," people have a less anxious reaction to the word and they are more willing to engage in the process. Change management typically is the term applied to companies that are underperforming and need immediate rectification of problems to bring about changed outcomes.

Transformations are more related to organizations that need to refine their practices, evolve, and improve to become greater organizations. These are two different applications and projects and both have their time and place in an organization, depending on what results are in the top and bottom line.

A tough call to face in some change situations

For any organization, the hardest project delivery is to bring about change in a distressed organization using the existing executive. This person has provided the direction of what has caused the current situation to be in place and now in his or her mind has to admit, that was wrong and we are now going in another direction. Likelihood that admittance will occur is minimal. Many executives lose credibility when they do a change of direction with the company they have managed for a number of years in the past.

The transformation can often be highly stressful for all individuals involved and in many cases the executive becomes a victim of the change process. Change can be a most traumatic affair in an organization or it can go relatively smoothly. It depends on how it is delivered. If you place a time frame on it that is relatively short in which to achieve results, say 90–120 days, then the term "change" moves to the term "revolutionize." It is a high-pressure experience without an ounce of room for error without significant negative impact in the sales organization—not a task for an inexperienced person to attempt. It takes a different type of leadership that can be confrontational to many people, as the timelines place enormous pressures through the business. Many executives that do elect to take this option fail, and organizations suffer even deeper pain than what was in place before they started. Failed projects are the death of many businesses.

Embracing transformation from within

Becoming a world-class sales organization is about transformation. An existing executive can announce a transformation and gain even higher credibility in the organization. Transformation for improvement and demanding high standards are positive and engaging for most people. Transformation is improvement, and everyone that accepts companies need to continually improve.

Radical changes may be made depending on the maturity of your sales organization, but that should not have the trauma associated with short time-frame change. You are there to lead and guide people through a project that ensures improvement for everyone involved.

Getting the timing right

Establishing the timeline is important. If you place too long a time frame on the project, then it is seen by others in the organization not as a transformation; it's just a project someone is amusing himself or herself with that will most likely derail. The organization will get focused on another subject or issue, putting the transformation on hold. In sales organizations with cultural problems, the sales team and others in the organization have plenty of time to find the gaps and play the diversionary games to achieve the project's derailment.

If the time frame is too short, then the pressure is too great for many to bear and you are in a cultural change process that may verge on being a revolution. If you get the timing right, then you will succeed.

The primary task that is most important is to judge correctly the depth of the issues and number of tasks to be addressed and how many can be done simultaneously. Only when that is known do you have a reasonable timeline to expect. This comes back to having a sound review initially and setting out the project plan of what needs to be achieved and in what order.

You also need to put into the equation the abilities of the sales organization and how much they need to improve to reach the established standards. This will also affect the timeline.

What I have seen over the years is that most people either judge too short a time frame or far too long. Some business consultants indicate that it takes up to three years for change to occur. I would say they are looking for a very long assignment (or employment) that will ultimately fail. The timeline is not realistic to the market.

What I can say is that for the sales organization, anything over twelve months is just an amusement keeping a manager occupied. I have not seen a transformation project that cannot be delivered in under twelve months for sales organizations.

Who is on the bus with the driver

The key to making a transformation happen is having the right people lead the project. A person experienced in project management and completion is the most important factor in the process—someone who is accountable and can be relied upon to monitor, measure, and manage the project to the desired outcomes, a person who is a respected member of the business and respected within the business by everyone at the executive level. The person will be reliant on their support to ensure the project can be delivered.

Another significant key to your success is that all senior executives and managers who are involved in the project must be working to the same goals, with no disparity of ideas or process. People must be acutely aware of the impact of their statements and conversations. Even the most innocent or off-hand comments can prompt barriers to the transformation project being successful.

Sales individual and teams involved in transformations and change look for those cracks between the executive team members where they can find reasons to slow down or even stop the change process. Do they do this intentionally? Certainly not. It's just a natural reaction to being asked to change as they unconsciously exercise their options before taking on board the new processes. People are looking for the least amount of change to affect them.

For companies who do not place enough emphasis on the collective group of executives being in agreement (even if behind the doors they debate strongly), here is a little tale that we see many times over in the market. It is the story of what happens to people through the change process, despite their best-laid plans.

Who Blocked the Change Process?

Richard was the CEO of a high-profile business that was struggling to achieve results on the sales front. Certainly, the image of the business in the market did not represent what was actually happening behind the scenes. The organization was about sixty people strong and some personnel had been with the organization for over ten years, while others were quite new to the business.

The people on the whole were young, vibrant individuals with high-energy input into the business and how it operated.

The board of directors was a group of high-profile businesspeople who had each been successful in their own right, each from different backgrounds but all with a similar approach to selling. The selling style was very traditional and focused heavily on closing hard on deals. They were in a business that required a different selling style that was more consultative; therefore, it took them into foreign territory. The customers would not accept the old style of selling and were moving on.

Richard decided that it was necessary to embark on a change program in the sales area of the business. At the next board meeting, he presented his thoughts to the board. They were all in agreement and noted that it should be a priority to improve the cash flow and profitability in the business. The change was definitely necessary if the business was to achieve returns back to shareholders.

In an unusual situation, one of the other board members, Max, also worked in the business on day-to-day basis alongside Richard. Max was in a management role of one of the divisions within the business that had its own sales organization. Max was a strong person who had always led from the front and was well-known in the industry for his business prowess, though he lacked people management skills. His management style was antiquated and more like the Gordon Gecko (Wall Street) of the world. Max sought people who would follow him without question.

Richard, on the other hand, was a collaborative leader and sought to have everyone's buy-in. He was a strong team builder in good times and had a high level of engagement with the employees. Richard called a meeting with everyone and advised on what was going to happen over the coming month for the sales organization. He requested that everyone support the process and asked for everyone's commitment to the change. This included managers of production, finance, and all other areas of the business.

As they moved forward in the change process, many things started to be uncovered. They installed new reporting processes that started to pinpoint issues, not only in the sales organization but also in the costing of products that were being taken to market.

Over the next few months it became obvious that the depth of problems was great and was spread across a number of areas, all contributing to less profit. Richard was struggling to come to grips with the issues that were uncovered; line managers were looking on and decided their input was vital; and many believed they had all the answers on how to achieve the outcome they all desired. They were enthusiastic and wanted to assist, but none were experienced in change management and they were acting on passion rather than experience.

The business started to fragment, with small cultures developing across groups of people who were seeking support for their individual beliefs as to how the business should be operated. Richard had an open-door policy and was discussing each of those beliefs with the people, but then not bringing the person back to the intended line of change that was required. Richard was in fact endorsing the subcultures by allowing them to foster their own directions and thoughts to the point that no one was engaged with the original change program. Their focus shifted to the management of the change rather than the outcomes required.

From the outset, Max had retained an arm's-length attitude to the change and did not want to be seen to be part of the process. He was a person who liked to be in control and where that control was not available, he declined to be involved in the activities.

As the people started to fragment and the pressure started to rise in the business, it was obvious that many people had been failing in their roles over a longer period of time and that the sales problem was a result of many issues and not the cause. People were looking to cover their performance issues and focus the attention on others. No one really knew which way to go forward. People started to look for strength to guide them through it. Richard's collaborative style was not providing that strength and it was not showing the staff a way forward. Interestingly, no one wanted to be the leader. They were only willing to share their thoughts on what could be done and the misgivings of others. All they needed was an ear to allow them to vent their thoughts regularly.

When the line managers approached Max to discuss generally what was happening, he began expressing his opinions. Those opinions were taken as strength, and the organization personnel started to follow Max, believing he would take them through the problems. Richard became more and more withdrawn as he was unable to bring about the change. Max allowed line managers to take on the role of advisors to him in the process and be leaders in their own small groups they had developed. He supported their activities, even though he was not actively involved in the process. He held them in the front line while he provided his opinions in the back lines.

The business suffered as it became more internally focused, and a war broke out over who was leading the change. Sales suffered and many people went into protection mode. Richard withdrew completely and based himself at home. Max announced he was taking control of the business and in true authoritarian style started shouting orders of what had to be done. People started to scatter and hide, some even leaving, as he used their information and knowledge from the previous months to drive home his points when necessary. He announced to everyone that he knew from the outset that the change process was doomed and that he had never really supported it. He then began to remove about half of the people to cut costs.

Who had blocked the change process? Max. The line managers contributed, but Max's lack of buy-in from the outset placed the business on the wrong path. When the organization had the choice of either putting its shoulder to the wheel and driving forward or finding a way to cop out, Max opened a side door and said, "Come this way!"

The alternative is a transformation project that recently was undertaken where the executives were given a timeline of twelve months by the board to deliver the outcomes. The project required the sales organization to be transformed to a highly competitive sales force as they were suffering loss of market share and profits, and morale was falling rapidly across the organization.

The Collective "Yes"

Peter was a highly regarded sales manager in the organization and had been with them for over ten years. He had started as a technical person and moved his way up the corporate ladder to the role of sales manager and had held the position for about one year before the global financial crisis hit. The business was successful and trading throughout North America.

In the following twelve-month period the business was battered and bruised by the market and competitors, and the business was on a very fast downward trend.

The executive called a meeting and discussed what was the best approach to move forward. The executive team contemplated all the usual discounting, cost cutting, and financial-related tasks but their major concern was how the business would look at the other side once all that was completed. Would they be able to sustain themselves in the market?

Peter communicated his concerns that downsizing the team was not actually going to increase sales and that certainly nothing was being discussed that made them more competitive as a team. They would be doing the same thing in twelve months' time with less people and less market share. He believed the opportunities were in the market, but the problem was they were just not winning them.

The executive agreed there was validity to his statements, and they all agreed to explore options that were more focused on improvement than cost-cutting. The dramatic change was going to be based on improvement for the business.

We reviewed the business and identified an array of points that could be developed and improved that would have significant impact on their competitiveness as an organization and how they operated as a sales organization. There were some elements that were quite explosive for executives to read, as they went to the core of what some people believed—they would need to change their beliefs for the business to move forward.

They decided to book a weekend away as an executive team to clear their heads, look objectively at the situation, and devise the next step. We were not involved in the weekend but it was reported back to us the following week that it contained some very heated debates and some serious analysis of their individual motivations, and they all put their cards on the table. They agreed that the project was required and would be of significant value to the organization. They agreed that the timing was critical and they disagreed on a number of smaller points within the project.

The best agreement of all is they decided to keep a strong face to the business, demonstrating agreement, and would only discuss issues offsite, where staff had no reference of what issues were being discussed. A united front was to be shown and demonstrated to the staff at all times.

A timeline was established for each and every task, with good project management principles applied. The sales manager was very detail-minded and able to work the project through. He looked to the other executives to support him where the project affected other areas of the business too.

A timeline of nine months was established (being the balance of that financial year). The executive communicated the requirements to the organization as a group and advised that there would be monthly meetings held with all the executive and staff confirming the progress and wins. They invited everyone to be engaged in the transformation and confirmed their availability to meet on an individual basis for those with concerns along the journey.

At the end of the three-month period, the business had made significant inroads and was transforming growth in the top line and evidence of the bottom line improvement. Meetings were being held with the individuals assisting and supporting them through the process, and all executives held their united line.

At the end of six months, the top and bottom line had improved, the pipeline was full of great projects, and their win rate was increasing rapidly. The sales manager was focused on the details and kept everyone focused on the right things that contributed to the moneymaking line. The open communication continued as people were gaining momentum with how the new organization operated.

At the end of the nine months the transformation was complete. The results were in and sales revenue and profits were up. As the rest of the market had deteriorated, they had achieved growth. A celebration party was held and the board members all arrived to congratulate the company as a whole.

The board members made inquiries to various individuals as to their thoughts on why the transformation was so successful.

The answer consistently came back that it was due to the open communication with the executives so they understood what was going on. The united team gave them enormous confidence that the company knew what they were doing and that they should follow; and they were informed of each of the changes and why it was needed, and the value to everyone that it affected.

The business continues to grow to this day.

Lessons can be learned from both those scenarios of what to do and what not to do in a transformation.

Chapter 24:

Don't be Yesterday's Company in Tomorrow's World

The decision to embark on a transformation is driven by the market and by a company's ability to stay competitive. Specifically, it is the executive's expectations of market share and the executive's own competitiveness—whether he or she wants to be number one in their industry. A market leader.

If the executive's motivation is increasing profit and shareholder returns, then a transformation makes sense if the results are delivered in the top and bottom line.

As you reflect on your organization in your mind, you may have identified elements of the sales organization, or even the whole, that can be transformed—new processes and methods—to drive it forward. You may have been alerted by some of the problems described in this book, and it could be that the marketplace is sending you a clear message that you need to be making decisions for the future.

Today or tomorrow?

Some organizations will feel more pressure than others based on their experience through the global financial crisis. Some will be convinced that the need for change is now and it is about deciding on the best path forward. Others will be thinking they seem to be holding ground at the moment and saying, "We will see which way the market turns." The decision an executive makes will only be known to be good or bad in hindsight.

Top-performing executives are often those that can grasp opportunities by making fast decisions and can calculate risk quickly as they make those decisions. That is a skill gained from broad experience that provides them with insight. These experienced people have a sense of when a decision needs to be made and make decisions before the problems have escalated. They can divert issues in a sales organization and can, in a sense, read what is going to happen. These organizations have the smoothest transition through a transformation as they typically get the timing right of when to start.

At the other end of the scale, there are those that become frozen and can't make the necessary decisions. They are looking continually to find signs that say, "take the left road," instead of looking for the signs that say "take the right road." They seek a lot of signals from the market before they take action and often by the time they see enough signals, it is really getting a little too late. They are reactionary executives that are more comfortable with the current situation that making any form of changes.

They are somewhat like the frog in the pot of water. For those unfamiliar with the reference, the story goes that if you put a live frog in a pot of water and turn on the heat slowly, as the water warms up the frog will remain in the water and not attempt to jump out. They literally sit there and get cooked alive. They don't do the obvious and jump out of the hot water.

People have patterns of behavior in their decision making. Some have patterns of behavior that bring about successful decisions, and others unfortunately have decision-making behaviors that cause further problems. Making a timely decision on when to embark on a transformation to a world-class sales organization is an important decision. It is not about reaching for great heights with a sales organization; in fact, it about being competitive in the new world that has become the new marketplace that everyone is operating in.

It is very easy to be caught up in your own world and not realize how fast the rest of the world is changing around you. This story of a business that was well-known to us is an excellent example of these different worlds.

Living in another world

George was the director of a long-standing instrumentation business that had enjoyed being a market leader for many years and was to many an institution in its specialist field. The organization was selling to a well-defined target market and over the years had sought and secured the best products in the world to supply that market. George benefited from the organization's success in both lifestyle and earnings. The business was strong and robust.

Six years ago, George contacted us to discuss whether his sales force needed some training; he was convinced they needed only a little brush-up of skills.

They were still doing well in the market, but he felt a little brush-up would help to sustain their relationships with customers. The small team of about six or seven who reported directly to George had been with him for a number of years. They knew the market, knew the customers, and had very strong relationships with them. The team attended a public program with a number of other organizations and throughout the training claimed that their relationship was the reason the customers dealt with them and that they did not really need to sell them.

The team were dedicated to relationship selling and declared that any other selling style was for other industries. Their sales results demonstrated they were right. George trusted his salespeople and relied on their representations of how the market was running. He managed them with a hands-off approach, as he had many other things to focus on in the business and he knew they would keep him informed and let him know if they had any problems. They did not need systems, as they all knew what was required and just got on with it.

Recently, a member of our client service team rang George to alert him to a new service and see how he was travelling. George said that things had changed and he had downsized. They only had a couple of salespeople now and were winding the business down.

Upon hearing this feedback, I started to read over the notes on the database from communications with George over the years. About two years after the training, George had lost a couple of salespeople and the new ones were not working out. According to George, it was hard to get salespeople and certainly ones who wanted to stay in the industry. It was an industry problem. George did not want to invest in them until they proved their worth to the organization; otherwise, it was wasted money.

About twelve to eighteen months later, George said that the team had been reduced even more and he was still finding it hard to get good salespeople. His products were still in demand and the internal sales team were keeping the relationships sound. The top line had gone down, but through effective management they were still making great profit. The industry was going through change and everyone else was feeling it. His competitors were also feeling the pinch.

George's decisions and beliefs had assisted him in managing the downsizing of the business to literally half its original size. It seemed odd that the business he was in was not excelling, as the products remained high-demand.

On looking at others on our databases that were in similar industries, we quickly identified another organization that was a competitor of George's organization. Out of curiosity, I telephoned the director, Andrew, and he reported excellent growth: the sales team had increased from three to fifteen people. They had been investing in all their people and opening new markets; their revenue had increased from $2.5 million to $20 million. They had acquired new products and were on a strong upward trend.

I asked Andrew whether he knew George. He confirmed that he did and said that George's organization used to be a force in the industry, but had failed to keep up with the market. It was a shame, as it was a good market, but the business had downsized and was not really worth purchasing now, because it did not have any value that could contribute to the current market.

George is now out of the market and the value of the business turned out to be stock and fittings only. The customers were raided by competitors, and the salespeople that remained were not even taken up in the industry. They were out-of-date and their practices did not fit into more competitive environments.

Making timely and informed decisions is often the measure of any executive or leader. Good decisions made at the right time can define what an organization will experience in the future. Poor decisions can certainly bring about many internal struggles and challenges that go to the core of the organization's profitability.

Demanding excellence or world-class standards in a sales organization is no longer as idealism but rather a reality of what will ensure you remain competitive now and in the future. It is a company's insurance policy against changing markets and competitor behavior. Those standards will define how the organization will be enabled to respond to market and competitor changes.

Executives and sales managers need to give consideration to the state of their sales organization. Does the sales organization demand best-practice or operate on legacies that served them well in by-gone eras? Is the company reliant on the product as their point of difference and are leaving the sales organization sadly lagging behind? Importantly, can the organization grow and what steps are being made to drive that growth into the future profitability?

The world is changing around you, and you need to consider how your organization will keep up with those changes. How big is the step you need to take not just keep up with the changing markets, but lead the market against your competitors? Are you taking small steps when in fact you need to be taking quantum leaps forward to ensure your position in the market in the future?

The decisions you make today will define what your organization is tomorrow.

Epilogue

This book may have provided you with some insight into how other companies are seeing their market, their sales organizations, and their priorities for the years ahead. The objective of this book is to provide executives to have a reference point of the experience of other companies and to understand that should you be faced with challenges in your business, you are not alone. Many companies have been affected by the global financial crisis, and many will continue to be for the years ahead.

One thing for sure is that the crisis is not going to end quickly and cleanly. It has a long tail that will continue to shift for the foreseeable future. The market has taught us many lessons over the past few years; some of those have been good lessons and others not so good.

Companies have emerged as smart companies with new business models and will see the crisis as a pivotal moment in the history of their businesses—the point at which new success was discovered for them. Others will emerge battered and bruised and breathing a sigh of relief that they survived in some form or manner.

The decisions that executives make will have deep and enduring impacts on organizations, even if the decision is to make no decision at all.

Through the examples of what other companies are doing and how they are addressing the required changes, you may gain some foresight into actions you need to be taking and priorities you need to be setting for your organization.

You may have already been a victim of one of the other stories where companies suffered through decisions made, and hopefully the other stories will contribute to your not repeating those same mistakes.

I hope this book has given executives and sales managers the confidence to take that next step to transform the sales organization and has given you insight into what needs to be done. There are many rewards that are available to you when you take the right road to build the most effective sales organization in the world.

Good decisions are only known in hindsight.

May your decision today support you tomorrow.

Case Study
Industry Practice versus Best Practice

Industry: Printing

Structure: National organization with head office and
               manufacturing facilities and state sales offices.

Turnover: $75,000,000 per annum

The print industry is an industry that is very reliant on industry practice being a mainstay in its decision making and strategic planning, with potentially more emphasis placed on industry practice than in most other businesses. The companies follow a style of industry legacy, and companies follow along with those that are perceived to be industry leaders or innovators in their field. That may be a sound move for innovation of printing processes but does not translate well into all operational practices.

This particular business had attempted several price rises in an attempt to remedy its profitability and made the obvious cutbacks within the business supply chain and overhead management. SFI was asked to review the mature business that was suffering from negative profit for the previous years and was now in a process of further downsizing staff numbers in the manufacturing and operational side of the organization. The business was now in permanent shrinkage and would continue to shrink in size and not necessarily achieve profit through that process.

The sales force included forty-five salespeople and support people with a ratio of one to one of salesperson to support person in most regions. This was unheard of in other industries and it certainly set off alarms that the processes within the company warranted such a high human capital requirement for serving customers.

If you look at how the business had evolved, most of the pre/post sales activities were related to finding a competitive advantage in the market. They had adopted many of the actions that would remove tasks from customers, thereby streamlining their print acquisition and management. In theory the moves were good but on review of the profitability, they had made no or very little adjustment to their internal processes to ensure long-term profitability. Needless to say, that was the reason we were engaged—to find the profit in the top and bottom line and to establish how to transform the sales organization.

Like many print companies, they had moved to the model of large print runs being completed and stock being held on the customer's behalf. That stock was released on-demand from the customer, mainly to government departments and large corporations, and the role of pre/post sales was to ensure that stock levels were maintained and dispatches were made timely. The customers communicated with the salesperson, who provided the answers to all their queries and managed their accounts personally. Relationships were deemed a high priority in the business. The support personnel in the pre/post sales areas provided extensive reporting to the customers on stock levels and order movement, and prompted them for more ordering when required. The customer and vendor were true business partners and one relied on the other for the total print solutions.

The management of the company was adamant that this was how the business must be operated, and it met all the customer's requirements. The customers were reported to be well serviced and customer reviews supported that assertion by management. The issue was, however, that though the customers were pleased, the profit was disappearing completely. Management were very fixed in their minds over how the structure of the sales organization should be.

During our review process we quickly uncovered a level of customer dissatisfaction that was evidenced from frontline sellers through to support mechanisms. The company was difficult for customers to work with even though it had all the offerings in place.

Through the analysis of capacity planning of the outside or field sales division and through deep analysis of their tasks, costs of operation, and budgets/quota, it was identified that the business was operating in excess of 40 percent under capacity. The human capital requirements of the business were severely underutilized even though they all reported they were busy each day and observed to be very busy on initial visual observation.

The direct cost to the business in human capital costs was $1,600,000 of excess salaries and bonuses. This was direct cash loss to the business, and it occurred through a combination of legacy and poor management.

The review further uncovered some forty-two points of disparity over sales organization processes, procedures, and the way the salespeople operated in the field and internally in relation to the company strategy. These all had an indirect cost of unnecessary expenses and lost profit to the company through inefficiencies and incompetence. The customer base was focused on the top one hundred customers, with some one thousand other customers failing to have account plans and rankings. This was an opportunity cost that was being lost. The figure was dependant on the market and whether that level of market share could be taken from competitors.

The review further showed that budgets/quota must be increased by 22 percent across the team to warrant the salaries they were receiving. The cost of sales against budgets/quota was erratic and lacked any real financial computation. Salaries were paid based on perceived skill and longevity in the business rather than on fiscal calculation.

Through analysis of tasks and time allocation for the internal or inside sales personnel, balanced against customer requirements of services offered, it was identified that those tasks could be realigned, producing an additional 60 percent of their time being available. This was a large capacity for the business to free up and take on more business and communications with a deeper customer base.

The acquisition of new business would also resolve the issues in production of inconsistent production flow and underutilization of their facilities and machines. That change alone would contribute handsomely to the profitability.

The business case demonstrated that a combination of transformations was required that would realize a combination of increased capacity (opportunity) and cash profit.

Business Case for Transformation to a World-Class Sales Organization:

- Direct profit from removal of excess field sales personnel/ salaries: $1,600,000 or 2 percent EBIT, and maintenance of existing service model to customers.

- Realignment of sales tasks, removing duplication within the business service model: $795,000 or 1 percent EBIT.

- A direct saving of $2,395,000 or 3 percent, EBIT was achievable within twelve months, or increased budgets/quota of $16,500,000 gross revenue, with improved profitability as noted above.

Case Study

Reworked Over and Over Again

Industry:	Manufacturing for the construction industry
Structure:	National organization with head office and single manufacturing site and state sales offices in primary states
Turnover:	$50,000,000 per annum

The organization had been a small business for many years, with a focus on product development and reliability of products in the market. With a change of executives and growth strategies, the business was now growing at an expediential rate and expanding into new markets. The growth was being achieved through acquisitions being made of competitors, and growth rates were exceeding 35 percent per annum year on year.

As a manufacturing company, they imported raw materials to manufacture complex equipment with a high level of customization. The offering of equipment customization to their customers contributed to their growth. The owners of the company were very product driven, with a strong research and development team in place to continually support their position in the market. The manufacturing area was upgraded to newer purpose-built premises that provided them with the opportunity for planning and executing a lean environment. Considerable funds were invested into the manufacturing process, and the improvement was ten-fold.

The sales organization of the business was seen as an afterthought within the business, as the telephones literally rang with orders no matter what they did. With executives' lack of priority on the sales organization, the management of the sales team's performance was laissez-faire. The sales capability of the individuals was so poor, they would be unemployable in most other companies.

The business was profitable despite the poor sales efforts; however, with the high costs of expansion and a shift in the market due to the financial crisis, no longer could the business absorb unnecessary costs as the profit margins came under scrutiny. Various individuals within the business had made attempts of change, but each had failed. Those attempts had created a fortress attitude in the sales organization, both in the central office and the remote offices.

The review of the business was conducted to ascertain the extent of the cultural problems, the operational tasks of the sales organization, and their impact across the entire business. The most significant problems that were identified early were communication issues, data entry issues, internal processing issues, and task allocation issues. Each of these areas created what is referred to as rework, or the unnecessary repetition of a task to remedy an error. In this operation, each time an order was incorrectly entered, the ramification through the business was like a tsunami. What started as a small incident quickly amplified to a major problem for the business, with a high cost-to-remedy ratio associated—particularly in the area of customized goods, where scrap became an escalating problem for production.

The problems were not unknown to the business, and they had previously attempted to remedy the problems through improved systems and implementation of a new ERP system. The implementation of the new ERP system was treating the problem and not treating the cause. Nor was it addressing the originators of the problem and all the contributing factors. In the case of this manufacturing company, the error level was analyzed to be to $1,035,000 in lost cash profit. This equated to 2 percent EBIT being lost unnecessarily within this business each year.

On reviewing the operational processes and identification of all the contributing factors, there was some thirty-eight points that required addressing with a high level of human capital-related issues. There was an expected lack of measurements in the business and reporting by sales personnel. Management did not use reports and measurement to manage any element of the sales organization other than sales revenue. Capacity planning demonstrated the salespeople's productivity to be under 18 percent, with a cost that was triple salary-to-margin ratio.

In a review of opportunity cost due to the dysfunctional behavior of the sales team through poor management, the extrapolation on this manufacturing business was equivalent to 7 percent EBIT, or $3,622,500 profit.

The analysis of the business demonstrated that in a transformation of sales personnel being focused on direct revenue generation, and operational requirements being managed by operations personnel, the opportunity existed for the company for a further 28 percent growth on existing levels. Analysis was required to be completed on market capacity to support that additional growth, or internal adjustments needed to be made to human capital in order to have focused individuals on tasks and the downsizing of the sales team.

To remedy the problem internally would not transpire, as the management was part of the problem and not the cure. Our recommended project manager had extensive knowledge in cultural change and delivery of detailed projects. His background supported a well-measured and task-orientated work flow that needed to be installed to remove the profit chasm. It was expected that it would take twelve months for the full value to be realized from the transformation.

Business Case for Transformation to a World-Class Sales Organization:

- Direct profit from removal of rework actions: $1,035,000 EBIT.

- Realignment of sales tasks: 7 percent EBIT or $3,622,500 profit.

- Additional savings from improved sales structure and processes to be confirmed once structures and processes established in the project.

Case Study
Capacity planning versus legacy planning

Industry: Agricultural

Structure: National organization with head office, state and
                 district offices.

Personnel: Approximately 2,500 in Sales Organization

The organization was a long-standing industry leader with many decades of history in the agricultural markets. The business was diversified in its services offered and was well regarded by its customers. The business's primary value proposition was the knowledge and expertise of the frontline sales-related personnel and their ability to work with the customers over the longer term in servicing all their agricultural requirements. All personnel were renowned for their longevity of employment within the organization, and personal relationships with the customers was seen as a primary point of difference over their competitors. There was little staff turnover and the business was profitable, but the ever-pressing requirement to deliver more returns to the shareholders.

The business contained legacies that were deeply entrenched into the culture of the organization, and practices that had supported its operation for many years but never examined to what degree they were really supporting the business into the future. What we do know is there is a sense of comfort for many people in processes that have been seen across a number of different businesses within an industry. They are tried and true and reliable, and they get the job done. The people working in the business can follow a set of standards and the outcomes are known (with some degree of variance) and accepted by all. It's referred to as the culture of the business and the legacies of the past.

On conducting initial reviews with the managers, we asked them to provide feedback of the major barriers they had to overcome as leaders of their business units.

There was a resounding cry of "understaffed," and this quickly gathered momentum when managers gathered together. They were unable to deliver the outcomes required without more staff and there was a company freeze on increased head count. There was no belief that forecasted revenues could be achieved based on the current personnel.

We set about a process of evaluating first and foremost the capacity of the sales organization and where potential profit may be uncovered. Through a series of analysis tools and calculations of the head count performance standards, it was uncovered that the business units were predominately over staffed. Without making any changes to territories, role requirements, or structure within the sales organization, there was additional performance capacity of 32 percent available across the board that could be effectively utilized for improving top-line business performance. This was of course subject to market share being available to support additional growth.

This revised performance standard would be at a comfortable operational standard for all sales personnel, allowing for their various geographical complications. To achieve this increased capacity required changes to the management style being applied and systems which would need to be driven by the business unit management.

With further analysis it was uncovered that due to the legacy of personnel, the quota/budgeting process had serious fluctuations that were demonstrating that 17 percent of budgets/quota were below minimum requirement, causing cost of sales to increase unnecessarily. This directly affected human capital costs for each business unit. With the adjustments to budget/quota, the business had the opportunity to realize up to a 4 percent decrease in cost of sales salaries. Across 2,500 sales personnel this was estimated to be $32,000,000 in additional net profit.

The review further uncovered some twenty-nine points of disparity over sales organization processes and procedures and how the salespeople operated in the field and internally in relation to the company strategy.

Due to the organizational size, several project managers were installed to map out identified areas of improvement in the sales organization and drive the transformation.

It would be a task to bring about the transformation due to the legacies, but these changes would realize more shareholder return with some hard work all round.

Business Case for Transformation to a World-Class Sales Organization:

- Cash profit increase on realignment of budgets/quota: $32,000,000.

- Increased performance capacity of 32 percent, equated to 2.2 percent increase in EBIT.

To connect with the author:

www.adelecrane.com

LinkedIn:
https://au.linkedin.com/in/adelecrane

Twitter:
https://twitter.com/adele_crane

To read more from Adele Crane, subscribe to:

Blog:
http://www.adelecrane.com/category/business-blog/